Migration and the New Europe

Significant Issues Series

SIGNIFICANT ISSUES SERIES papers are written for and published by the Center for Strategic and International Studies.

Series Editors: David M. Abshire
                          Douglas M. Johnston

Director of Studies: Erik R. Peterson

Director of Publications: Nancy B. Eddy

Managing Editor: Roberta L. Howard

Associate Editor: Donna Spitler

This publication is based on a CSIS Conference on the Security Dimensions of International Migration in Europe, held in Taormina, Sicily, April 1–3, 1993.

❖   ❖   ❖

Center for Strategic and International Studies
1800 K Street, N.W., Suite 400
Washington, D.C.   20006
Telephone: (202) 887-0200
Fax: (202) 775-3199

Migration and the New Europe

Edited by *Kimberly A. Hamilton*

Foreword by *Robert E. Hunter*

THE CENTER FOR STRATEGIC & INTERNATIONAL STUDIES
Washington, D.C.

Significant Issues Series, Volume XVI, Number 2
© 1994 by the Center for Strategic and International Studies
Washington, D.C.   20006
All rights reserved
Printed in the United States of America

Library of Congress Cataloging-in-Publication Data

Migration and the new Europe / edited by Kimberly A. Hamilton ;
foreword by Robert E. Hunter.
        p. cm. -- (Significant issues series, ISSN 0736-7136;
v. 16, no. 2)
        Includes bibliographical references.
        ISBN 0-89206-214-2
        1. Europe--Emigration and immigration. I. Hamilton, Kimberly
A. II. Series.
JV7590.M524 1994
325.4--dc20   93-32176
                                                                  CIP

JV
7590
.M5173
1994

Contents

3

Shaping a Multilateral Response to Future Migrations   37

Jonas Widgren

4

Involuntary Migration: Refugees in the New Europe   56

Kathleen Newland

5

Migration and Economic Intervention   72

Sidney Weintraub and Georges A. Fauriol

About the Contributors

Georges A. Fauriol is a senior fellow at the Center for Strategic and International Studies (CSIS) and director of the CSIS Americas Program, which engages policymakers in Canada, the United States, Mexico, Latin America, and the Caribbean in issues of common concern. Before joining CSIS he was associated with the Foreign Policy Research Institute, the U.S. Information Agency, and the Inter-American Development Bank.

Kimberly A. Hamilton is an adjunct fellow at CSIS and is currently pursuing a doctorate in sociology at Brown University. She was associate director of the International Economic and Social Development Program at CSIS, where she developed the CSIS project on the security dimensions of international migration in Europe as well as an expert working group on U.S. policy concerning the HIV/AIDS pandemic.

Robert E. Hunter is the U.S. ambassador to NATO. Before assuming that post, he was vice president for international politics and director of European studies at CSIS. His previous positions include director of Middle East affairs and director for West European affairs on the National Security Council.

Sören Jessen-Petersen has worked for the Office of the United Nations High Commissioner for Refugees (UNHCR) since 1972 at UNHCR headquarters in Geneva, the UN Secretariat in New York, and field offices in Ethiopia, Egypt, and Zambia. He is currently the director of the executive office and external relations for UNHCR.

Tom Lantos has served in the U.S. House of Representatives since 1981. In addition to holding several committee assignments—he is a senior member of the Foreign Affairs Committee and vice chairman of the Subcommittee on Europe and the Middle East, among others—Representative Lantos is founder and cochairman of the

200-member bipartisan Congressional Human Rights Caucus, the umbrella human rights organization of Congress.

Kathleen Newland has been a consultant to the Office of the United Nations High Commissioner for Refugees since 1992 and is principal author of the UNHCR's 1993 report *State of the World's Refugees*. Ms. Newland, together with Lord David Owen, is a cofounder of Humanitas, a nonprofit educational trust devoted to promotion of debate on international humanitarian issues.

Demetrios G. Papademetriou is a senior associate at the Carnegie Endowment for International Peace. Before joining Carnegie's Immigration Policy Program, he was director of immigration policy and research at the U.S. Department of Labor and continues to chair the department's Immigration Policy Task Force as well as the Migration Committee of the Organization for Economic Cooperation and Development.

Sebastiano Vincelli is a member of the board of directors of the SED company, publisher of the *Gazzetta del Sud* daily, and a founding member of the Fondazione Bonino-Pulejo. A journalist by profession, he was elected to parliament in 1958 and reelected through four consecutive sessions. In 1978, he was elected to the Reggio Calabria Senate. He served as provincial and regional secretary of Italy's Christian Democratic Party and sits on the National Council.

Sidney Weintraub has been Dean Rusk Professor at the Lyndon B. Johnson School of Public Affairs at the University of Texas, Austin, and is a distinguished visiting scholar in the Americas Program at CSIS. Previous positions include senior fellow at the Brookings Institution, assistant administrator of the Agency for International Development, deputy assistant secretary of state for international finance and development, chief of the USAID mission in Chile under the Alliance for Progress, and chief of commercial policy in the State Department.

Jonas Widgren is director-designate of the International Center for Migration Policy Development in Vienna, which focuses on finding solutions to new migration challenges in the industrial world. Prior to that he was with the Office of the United Nations High Commissioner for Refugees, where he was coordinator for intergovernmental consultations on asylum, refugee, and migration policies in Europe, North America, and Australia, heading the Secretariat in Geneva.

Foreword

Robert E. Hunter

In every generation, it is tempting to see the problems of the moment as somehow unique, produced by current circumstances and requiring solutions based on analysis simply of the events themselves. Often lost is the historical dimension—what has gone before, how events reflect patterns from the past, and what can be borrowed from earlier experience to facilitate understanding. This appears to be the case in much analysis of migration in Western Europe, especially in relation to the future of security across the Continent. To understand what is happening today—and what might be done about it—requires first a bit of perspective.

Looking back to the origins of European security after World War II, we can see that "security" was always an amalgam of politics and economics—that is, of the structures of society. The Marshall Plan was a security act. It came two years before the signing of the North Atlantic Treaty, which itself was more about politics at the outset than about military issues. It was only with the Korean War that the Atlantic pact was thoroughly militarized, when the O was added to NATO in 1951. The Helsinki Final Act similarly paralleled this combination of politics and economics. Thus, if security in Europe in the modern age can be seen as primarily about the structure and success of societies—with the military as an adjunct to, or instrument of, a broader set of purposes—then this is true in spades today.

The West won a triple victory in the cold war. The victory not only was strategic, as in the first two world wars; it also entailed the

This foreword is drawn from Robert Hunter's remarks to the CSIS Conference on the Security Dimensions of International Migration in Europe, held in Taormina, Sicily, April 1–3, 1993, in his position as vice president of international politics and director of European studies for CSIS and before his appointment as U.S. ambassador to NATO. The views expressed here are his alone and do not necessarily represent those of the U.S. government.

most massive retreat in all of peacetime history, reflected in the collapse of Soviet power. Equally important, it was a validation—or at least an apparent validation—of Western attitudes toward politics and economics. In that sense, victory in the cold war represents a victory more profound than that of either world war. It has, however, also been followed by a triple challenge to providing security for Europe. These challenges are (1) the development of genuine pluralism in post-Communist societies, (2) the establishment of successful market economies, and (3) the resolution of corrosive ethnic, religious, and national disputes and conflicts in the former Soviet bloc.

Related to this cold war victory and the emergent triple challenge is the truly remarkable historical development represented by the European Community—the creation of what is, in essence, a "European civil space." The 12 EC countries, which are far more disparate in so many respects than were the 13 American colonies two centuries ago, have nonetheless abolished war as an instrument of politics among themselves. Within some of these states there are still conflicts, but among them they have—in part by design and in part by fortuitous circumstance—created this functioning European civil space. Thus, Europe is currently attempting to implement the fundamental idea, which finds its roots in the writings of Emmanuel Kant, that democracies do not wage war on other democracies. Ironically for some Americans, this idea has perhaps been most directly articulated in our times by Ronald Reagan. Taken to its logical conclusion, the idea implies that "security" in the future will be fundamentally and historically transformed beyond the classic balance-of-power framework into something far better and more enduring. We have yet to see whether the experience of West European democracies can be duplicated elsewhere. Indeed, that is the gamble today for security in Europe, stretching into the East.

In the United States, the future of Russia is regarded as the primary geopolitical and geostrategic issue. Other issues may emerge as central concerns—particularly if things go well in Russia. If things go badly, however, as during the cold war, events in Moscow and environs will be the riveting focus for security analysts. Remarkably, U.S.-Russian relations are no longer devoted to armies, arms control, and nuclear weapons. They are instead focused on how the West can assist Russia and the other members of the Commonwealth of Independent States (CIS), precisely for security purposes. Such assistance includes gaining control over at least the causes and effects of migration, if not migration itself.

Attitudes within the Western alliance with respect to the impact of migration on European security differ. There is a fault line, with the Germanics and Nordics on one side, the Latin peoples on the other. The former are concerned about people coming in from the East, the latter about inflows from the South. Western Europe thus has no single set of security concerns about migration, given these different ways of viewing those who come to visit, to work, or to live permanently.

The growing concern about migration in Europe has four dimensions germane to the new security framework. First, the "production" of migrants is linked to security concerns—whether, for example, a civil war in Russia might result in the further breakup of that federation and whether growing conflict between Russia and its neighbors might send people on the move. Even questions about nuclear weapons are involved—an area where we believe we have gone beyond the old confrontations of the past. Whether Ukraine gives up nuclear weapons relates very much to the stability of its relationship with Russia and the possibility for migrant-producing conflicts.

Second, the cultural impact of outsiders coming to Western Europe entails a series of issues that relate to both a classic and a new security agenda. In general, integrating these people within societies is far more difficult in Europe than in America. America was founded on an idea—and as soon as a person becomes an American citizen, he or she becomes a custodian of the corporate history of our nation, with all the ensuing rights and benefits. In Europe, with some exceptions, ethnicity to a great extent defines nations.

In Germany and France, integration issues have recently tested the legitimacy of governments to manage what has ultimately become competition for revenues and economic benefits. The competition for resources also has a major security dimension. Indeed, it has been argued that the Common Agricultural Policy is, in some ways, the biggest impediment to integrating the societies of the East. The same can be said for North-South transfers of and competition for resources. In both cases, if western European states take some responsibility for what happens economically in the countries that are producing migrants, they will help to determine the degree to which this competition becomes a security problem.

Third, in the classic security sense, the capacity of allies to work together to preserve allied institutions will be sorely tested by what happens in the East and how developments there affect the West. Indeed, can we have turmoil in the East without its having a critical impact in Western Europe? The capacity of nations to work together in alliance and the attitudes we develop about engaging Eastern countries in Western notions of security-- and whether we do want and can have Eastern societies in our Western security institutions—will play an important role in future decisions. Can we, for example, think about broadening membership in NATO or the Western European Union (WEU) to include countries in turmoil, whose governments still have no settled relationship to their own populations?

Fourth, the capacity for security in Europe in the face of migration and similar population issues relates to peacekeeping and peacemaking. It is unlikely that Western institutions (e.g., the WEU, Franco-German Eurocorps, NATO) will be able to deal with that new dimension of security—the making and preserving of peace in troubled countries—without confronting issues relating to migration. In this regard, the fundamental failure in Bosnia poses a double bind. Before the United States was called upon, the European states failed in former Yugoslavia, in part because attitudes differed toward Yugoslavia's various regions as well as about what should be done. The double bind is that Yugoslavia's disintegration and the West's ineffectualness have increased migration, placed greater challenges on the West, and intensified pressure on the capacities of our institutions--multilateral as well as domestic.

In sum, the old distinctions drawn between strategists and humanists do not exist anymore in Europe. The distinction between security institutions and those for politics, economics, and human concerns also no longer exists. Unity of purpose and unity of action are required if we are going to meet the demands of the new security, including those posed by increasing migration into Europe from the East and the South.

Prefatory Remarks

Sebastiano Vincelli

The concept of an international conference to seriously examine the political, social, and economic effects of the migratory flux in Europe was born of collaboration between the Center for Strategic and International Studies in Washington, D.C., and the Bonino-Pulejo Foundation in Messina, Italy.

Assessing the growth of international migration resulting from strategic, economic, and political transformations in the former Soviet Union, Eastern Europe, and North Africa is of great importance to Europe's future security and stability. Through analyzing, evaluating, and confronting these fundamental issues, we hoped at the conference to redefine the international relations emerging from the end of the cold war and to describe the new international mechanisms, whether multilateral or bilateral, that will enable us to meet the challenges of transnational movements of people.

The recent great events in Europe and the end of opposing blocs of power have opened an unexpected possibility for peace and economic collaboration between East and West. At the same time, that collaboration has profoundly affected North-South relations, where we are witnessing the emergence of many Third World states from their former status of simple superpower "satellites." According to Luigi Perrone of the University of Lecce,

> If it is true that an era has ended, then this means that there is the need to rethink and to renegotiate everything, hopefully without causing catastrophic upheavals. The first thing to renegotiate is the redistribution of resources. This presently means the formulation of a new policy of cooperation on immigration. But, in order to put such policy into action, a new philosophy of life is needed.

Sebastiano Vincelli is a founding member of the Bonino-Pulejo Foundation, a member of the board of directors of the SED company, and publisher of the daily *Gazzetta del Sud*.

The need to develop a new "philosophy" was evident through-out the spring and summer of 1990, when thousands of individuals in successive waves crossed the Adriatic from Albania by whatever means possible to reach Italy. The Albanians expected and still expect much from Italy. Italy can play a meaningful role in Albania's development and stability simply by changing its philosophy of cooperation, not through charity (which creates expectations and dependence) but through productive economic intervention accom-panied by a change in immigration policy. The same is true for the Mediterranean Basin, where it is crucial to begin creating conditions for an orderly passage from the present economic anarchy—which makes this area one of the world's most volatile—to a balanced and integrated "pre-community" in the process of developing.

To date, European responses to international migration have proposed national and nationalistic solutions. Inevitably, such solu-tions have tended to acquire repressive and defensive features and produce protracted underdevelopment. The large migratory flows to Europe (which are expected to increase) will force European gov-ernments to intervene in housing, social services, and public safety, especially given current social tensions and outbreaks of overt and violent racism. Such intervention could add unbearable tension in a region already overpopulated and polluted.

Other factors will likely increase these migratory flows to Eu-rope. As Yves La Corte writes in *Geografia del sottosviluppo,*

> Categorizing a group of countries as Third World allows us to group together those nations that in the past have faced the same fundamental contradictions. These contradictions have on the one hand slowed the development of productive forces by directing these forces toward export activities which have tended to benefit a privileged minority connected to a foreign power. On the other hand, starting with the 20th century, they have caused extremely rapid demographic growth due to the elimination of the large mortality rate, while the birth rate did not diminish because of the persistence of some socio-cultural conditions.

The persistence of these conditions in the countries of origin, with rare exceptions, shows clearly that the migratory flux is destined to increase in the near future.

Population movements will not subside unless there is measur-able development in the countries of origin. The forced "choice," therefore, is that of economic intervention in poor countries. In this context, what the North can do becomes evident. Assistance must not only be part of an organized plan to transfer resources; it must also be distributed according to precise conditions and accompanied by actions that would guarantee the success of the program. The Marshall Plan is a useful point of reference, provided that its main points can be applied today. It is useful, for example, to remember that U.S. aid was conditioned on the European states' agreement to cooperate in its management, which eventually contributed to European integration.

The total elimination of immigration through aid and investments to developing countries is, however, not realistic. Migration will continue to have a domestic impact within Europe. Without an active commitment (political, civil, and cultural) from local communities, therefore, living together will often be a forced issue. Examples of this unhealthy situation can be found in the ethnic conflicts of nearby regions as well as in the intolerance and violence that have occurred in Italy. The final report of the 1984 United Nations International Conference on Population and Development observed that

> countries of destination must adopt measures aiming at protecting the fundamental human rights of all immigrants in their territory and at assuring the respect of their cultural identity. In addition, special measures need to be taken to promote the integration of the immigrant community and the population of the country of destination. In outlining their policies on international migration, the governments of the countries of destination must take into account not only the economic and social needs of the immigrants, but also the welfare of their families and the demographic implications of immigration.

It is therefore important to insist on better and more effective international cooperation and coordination to prevent discrimination, distortion, and division between the institutions and the procedures that concern foreigners.

Cooperation also means that the development and, most of all, the equilibrium of a certain area should not become the responsibility of a single country. Measures of cooperation can vary. Obviously one is financial help. Others include investment in the countries of origin, professional development, economic and technical cooperation, investment and placement of resources, and even the opening of borders to an agreed-upon number of immigrants, as negotiated with the countries of origin, to obtain their assistance in moderating migratory movements.

The cultural, political, and economic debate on international migration has greatly expanded, both in Italy and in the European Community. Confronted with the trend in migration, the European Community has generally tended to limit immigration by increasing controls and to carry out the process of integration with respect for human rights, not just with regard for economic factors. Yet even though Italy and the EC nations face the same situation and social problems and share the same objectives, they have not been able to coordinate their policies effectively. Now that the danger of the cold war has disappeared, every nation—although seemingly concerned with Maastricht or Europe—worries only about itself. Until the transnational movements of people can be understood in their global context, demanding coordinated responses and cooperative solutions, each country will continue to respond in its own way.

Introduction

Kimberly A. Hamilton

The increase in international migration across Europe—fueled by changes in East-West relations, demographic and economic pressures from the South, and continued armed conflict in the former Yugoslavia—has prompted a reevaluation of population movements within the context of European security. The volatility of that issue in a period of economic downturn, however, and the persistence of perceptions of crisis across the Continent have debilitated attempts at rational debate and coherent policy formulation. Finding solutions that eschew either complacency or hysteria is one of the greatest challenges facing the new Europe, its transatlantic partners, and international organizations mandated to manage refugee and migration flows.

This collection of commissioned papers results from a three-day conference in Taormina, Sicily, in April 1993, organized to tap the expert thinking of key foreign policy leaders from 16 countries, individuals from multilateral organizations at the forefront of the debate about migration, and leading journalists. The volume focuses on the steps necessary to anchor migration and immigration policies to a responsive and consistent framework. In addition to suggesting policy revisions, the authors have carefully outlined the impediments to crafting such policies, the challenges posed by global trends such as the internationalization of labor markets, and the limitations to the actions taken by sovereign nations. Although their emphases differ, all contributors define the *security* dimension broadly, appreciating the dynamics of economic, political, and social reactions as well as interventions.

Most important, the authors establish common threads of analysis that provide the basis for any serious investigation of the issue

Kimberly A. Hamilton is an adjunct fellow at the Center for Strategic and International Studies, where she developed the CSIS project on the security dimensions of international migration in Europe.

at the political level. In particular, the context or the conditions that continue to spur population movements—including civil unrest, environmental degradation, human rights violations, and economic and political upheaval—are viewed as more significant threats to stability than migration itself. In other words, the numbers often associated with recent migration in Europe must be disaggregated and perceived as part of a continuum of processes and provocations. Included here is the need to rethink our understanding of various "pull factors"—i.e., the mechanics of ethnic pathways, employment opportunities, and the role of firms in encouraging migration and influencing immigration policy.

These essays also emphasize the importance of intensifying co-ordinated responses to international migratory flows. Such effort includes coordinating popular messages to both receiving and sending countries and regions about the realities of migration, government policies, and reception at the border. It also involves greater exchange of information, resources, and expertise at the in-stitutional level, among governments, multilateral organizations, and grassroots affiliations. In the restructuring that must take place, there is a clear warning that protection for asylum seekers must not be lost, especially at a time of rampant political exploitation of the issue.

Finally, the analysts agree that South-to-North migration will be a prolonged and enduring challenge, demanding political and economic capital beyond current capacities. In this regard, the transatlantic partners can share important experiences about economic, political, and diplomatic tools useful in ameliorating migratory flows and about partnerships that can help to make such efforts successful. This will remain true even if managing migration becomes only a secondary or tertiary goal in overall conceptions of strategic planning.

Although the authors focus primarily on relations among sovereign states that encourage, limit, or shift migratory flows, issues such as conveying citizenship, the meaning of equality in the European context, and integration in the face of discrimination and stigmatization based on race, ethnicity, or religion are a powerful subtext throughout the essays. These topics were integral to the rich discussions among the participants in Taormina and clearly are increasingly salient to the general debate about redefining security.

Finally and perhaps most interesting for those who follow the ongoing dialogues on security, humanitarianism, and geopolitics, this volume represents a unique intersection of visions and roles within the international community. In the first of the five essays in this collection, Sören Jessen-Petersen focuses on refugee flows, particularly how the end of the cold war has narrowed the differences between concerns about international migration and regional security in Europe. Similar issues are raised by Kathleen Newland, who examines multilateral cooperation and schemes for preventing mass displacement in Europe. Demetrios Papademetriou approaches migration from the perspective of the receiving countries, assessing domestic policy responses—political and economic—that limit as well as enhance measures to manage immigration in the European context. Jonas Widgren's subject is fostering improvements in the overall international mechanism tasked with managing migration and refugee flows and, ultimately, with securing stability. In the final essay, Sidney Weintraub and Georges Fauriol analyze economic tools for the prevention of international migration, drawing distinctions between the European experience and that of the United States.

That these papers flow from a meeting organized by the Center for Strategic and International Studies, a research institution conceived at the height of the cold war, is indicative of the way in which emerging global challenges have permeated the thinking of traditional security institutions and are forcing much broader conceptualizations about what matters in the name of security. If, as is commonly held true in other arenas, security now is increasingly about coping with nonmilitary challenges, then circumstances likely to produce migration are also likely to remain constant reminders that future alliances and solutions will be broad indeed.

Acknowledgments

The Center for Strategic and International Studies is deeply grateful for the generous contributions from the Fondazione Bonino-Pulejo, the Embassy of Italy, the United States Institute of Peace, Ing C. Olivetti & Company, S.p.A., Robert Bosch Corporation, and Alitalia S.p.A. Their support and assistance throughout this project on the security dimensions of international migration in Europe have made this publication possible.

1

International Migration and Security: A Pragmatic Response

Sören Jessen-Petersen

Some 18 years ago in Helsinki, discussions of the human rights dimensions of the free movement of people opened the first tiny holes in the iron curtain. Indeed, it was the very movement of people that significantly helped to open the curtain some three years ago.

The movement of people has now come full circle and is seen by many in the West as a serious threat to the stability of our own societies. It should be agreed from the outset, however, that the threat comes, of course, not from the individuals moving across borders but from the causes that provoke mass movement. Our ability to manage and resolve the underlying problems that compel people to move will greatly influence the new world we are trying to build.

What are the dramatic changes that now juxtapose humanitarianism with regional security concerns, and how do we address them? This paper examines the changes that have caused international migration to be perceived as a security challenge as well as the pragmatic strategy proposed by the United Nations High Commissioner for Refugees (UNHCR) to address this challenge. The emphasis remains on refugees, the victims of involuntary migration. But the differences between refugees in *sensu stricto* and other migrants are becoming increasingly blurred, requiring a comprehensive response that embraces all groups compelled to move.

Before 1989

The Office of the UN High Commissioner for Refugees can almost be termed a creation of cold war politics. International support for victims of Communist persecution was indeed a motivating factor behind the establishment of the office in 1951. Flight from ostracized regimes in the East made the granting of asylum in the West an act of benevolence—and strategic interest. The need for protection against *refoulement,* or involuntary repatriation, was self-evident. In the 1950s, political interest and humanitarian concerns coincided.

In the 1960s and 1970s, the proxy wars of the cold war era and the heritage of colonialism compelled tens of millions in the developing world to flee. In the first 30 years of UNHCR's history, the convergence of political interest and humanitarian traditions allowed some 25 million refugees to become integrated in their countries of asylum, repatriate to newly independent countries, or resettle in a third country. In the late 1970s and the 1980s, proxy wars and a paralyzed international political climate made solutions to refugee problems elusive and forced UNHCR to engage in large, long-term, and expensive care and maintenance programs in poor countries of asylum in the Third World.

After 1989

It was hoped that those who could not benefit from a solution offered by the bipolar division of the world would reap the benefits with the end of the cold war. With some notable exceptions, such as Namibia, Cambodia, South Africa, Mozambique, and Eritrea, the end of the cold war led to everything but a solution to the refugee problem in many parts of the globe. Indeed, the problem intensified and spread as national, ethnic, and religious violence, previously held in check by authoritarian regimes, burst out with all the pent-up energy of 40 years of suppression. In the short term, particularly in Europe, liberalization, the granting of freedom of movement, led to an increase in the movement of people.

In 1984, approximately 100,000 persons moved from Eastern Europe to the West. The figure for 1989 was 1.2 million people. Asylum applications averaged around 30,000 a year for Western Europe in the 1970s. A decade later the number of applicants had surpassed 400,000 and by 1992 had reached 753,000. Worldwide today, there are 19 million refugees, between 20 and 25 million internally displaced individuals in refugee-like conditions, and 50 million migrants. The conflict in the former Yugoslavia alone provoked some 4 million people to flee their homes. More than 80 million people are on the move—possibly a greater number than ever before in history.

The vast majority not only originate from but also find sanctuary in the poorest parts of the globe. The smallest, poorest countries are frequently those that demonstrate the most extraordinary generosity. But although from a global perspective only a small percentage of refugee/displaced populations are in Europe, the scope of the problem—including the costs—and its implications seem enormous. More refugees and migrants are seeking to enter Europe than at any time since the massive postwar movements of people from the East. In contrast to the situation, however, the political and strategic value of granting asylum has diminished, while racial intolerance and nationalism within Europe are on the increase. These tensions are to some extent prompted and exacerbated by economic decline.

The causes for the massive increase in movement are complex. Resurgent nationalism is one motivating factor. From central and eastern Europe through the Caucasus to central Asia, new divisions are opening along ethnic and national lines, threatening the fragile architecture of a whole region and rousing fears of large-scale population displacement. On July 29, 1992, at the Geneva Ministerial Conference on Humanitarian Aid to the Victims of the Conflict in Former Yugoslavia, UN High Commissioner Sadako Ogata warned that what was happening in the former Yugoslavia could be a chilling omen for the former Soviet Union.

Poverty exacerbates nationalism. The income and employment differentials between the developed and the developing world have widened. Debt, recession, and impoverishment have intensified while malnutrition and populations continue to grow. At the same time, more wars are being fought than at any other time in history and mass violations of human rights are rampant. Is it a wonder that more people are on the move than ever before?

A major feature of the recent displacements is the very large number of people dislocated within their own frontiers. A further feature is the interrelatedness of the political and economic causes of displacement. Albania, Sri Lanka, and Haiti bear witness to the inadequacy of the easy distinctions of the past between economic migrants and individually persecuted refugees.

A vicious circle of poverty and political repression produces mass movement of peoples. Some individuals will qualify as refugees under the classical definition. Many more may be in need of protection, at least on a temporary basis, although they elude the 1951 Convention and 1967 Protocol definition of refugees, certainly when applied in its strictest sense and not in the spirit envisioned by its founders. A third group does not require protection, but the causes that provoke these people to move still need to be addressed by the international community.

The essence of the problem posed by today's population movements is that the numbers of displaced have continued to grow to the point that the international system is no longer able to deal with or manage the problem, at either the humanitarian or the political levels. We are, in a disquieting sense, back to the problems of the 1970s and 1980s. Problems are mushrooming everywhere while solutions are becoming increasingly elusive. More people are wanting to leave sending countries than hosting countries are willing to accept. Nationally the structures in place to receive aliens and refugees are overwhelmed. Widespread unemployment and recession create resentment against the foreign born. An often ill-informed public opinion plays a major role in determining national policies—especially where leaders forget or choose not to lead. Popular resentment and misinformation, particularly in Europe, have an impact on political will, resources, and public compassion.

Displacement appears to have come full circle in the 42 years of UNHCR history. Having started as a European problem and spread globally, it has come back to haunt its original home. The images of refugee camps in Europe, unknown since the late 1950s when the last camp was closed, and talk of "fortress Europe" when economic and political indicators point instead to "weakness" Europe, highlight the pressing nature of the problem of refugees and migration in Europe.

As the cradle of humanitarianism, human rights, and refugee law, Europe faces a particular dilemma: how does one preserve the principles of human rights, including the right to free movement, and traditions of humanitarianism without jeopardizing the security and social stability of societies?

The problem is not going to go away. Economic and social disparities will grow, forcing more people to move. An increasingly nonideological world means that conflicts are going to be rooted more and more in nationalistic, ethnic, and socioeconomic causes, making it all the more difficult to maintain the classical distinction between refugees, internally displaced persons, and migrants. The international scene is thus set for massive movements of the most vulnerable groups of people—across or within frontiers--yet the mechanisms for responding are increasingly outdated. The movements will continue to grow until, at both the political and humanitarian levels, the appropriate international strategies are devised to handle them.

Europe cannot cut itself off from the rest of world. Any attempt to confront the threat by building new walls, although possibly effective in the short term, will only aggravate the problem in the longer term, leading to new tensions as the distance grows between rich and poor, stable and unstable societies. The construction of a new wall along economic lines between North and South, East and West is a sure recipe for chronic global instability.

A Response Strategy

Our response to the challenge of displacement, migration, and refugees must be comprehensive rather than defensive. Building on our experience with comprehensive approaches in other regions of the world, the high commissioner is proposing a seven-point program based on three basic principles. First, responses must concentrate on the root causes of population movements. Second, the response must be as diverse as the varied, complex, and interwoven causes of departure. And third, as the world grows more interdependent, the response must go beyond national interests or short-term political considerations, lest short-term gains turn into long-term pains.

The first point in the high commissioner's strategy can be termed the reaffirmation of protection principles: Europe must reaffirm its readiness to provide protection to those who need it. In recent years in Europe, the implementing legislation derived from the 1951 Convention and 1967 Protocol, conceived of as a means of affording protection to those who need it, is being increasingly used in a manner contradictory to the spirit in which it was created—that is, as a means of excluding from protection those who are compelled to flee. The majority—some 60 percent—of those seeking asylum are not able to prove individual persecution as the cause of their flight, as is required under most European legislation. Many of them would, however, risk life and liberty if repatriated. They may be victims of violence, conflict, and chronic insecurity rather than a particular target of political persecution. Perhaps one way to recognize their peril is that, once admitted, such individuals, even if formally denied asylum, are usually not repatriated by the European states, but instead remain in a state of unhappy legal limbo.

Perhaps ironically, UNHCR looks after such persons in the developing world as refugees with the explicit support of European donors. Regional refugee legal instruments such as the 1969 Organization of African Unity (OAU) Convention as well as the Cartagena Declaration accept violence and political unrest as causes of flight. Legislators in Europe might draw a number of lessons from this more pragmatic definition of refugees, as well as from the traditional hospitality of Third World countries.

The failure of Europe to recognize this broader category of persons in need of protection and to interpret existing refugee legislation liberally has in turn fed European perceptions that asylum procedures are being abused. Such misperceptions have fueled xenophobia, which leads governments to adopt yet tighter policies. A way out of this vicious circle may be the notion of temporary admission to safety, which European governments have broadly accepted for those fleeing the former Yugoslavia. This allows victims of war and violence to find the sanctuary they badly need, while governments can afford to be more generous in the knowledge that their burden is temporary.

The second component in the strategy is the adoption of migration policies. Just as protection policies must address those fleeing war and persecution, migration policies should be developed to cope with those moving for economic and social reasons.

Many demographers and economists believe Europe would benefit from increased levels of immigration. But the pressures of apparently uncontrolled migration, coupled with uncertainty over future trends and numbers, have produced a siege mentality in Europe that encourages the tightening of controls. Would-be immigrants therefore see asylum as a way of avoiding immigration controls. With no other doors open, those seeking entry to better their economic and social situation use the asylum door. The number of "abusive" claims—meaning not relevant to asylum—has increased, bringing asylum procedures to the verge of collapse. A judicious mixture of asylum and migration policies is required. Canada and the United States, being more open toward, and experienced with, immigration, have not until now experienced the same dramatic difficulties that Europe is encountering with asylum seekers.

The third element of the strategy is information. Information is an essential element in any strategy to manage population movements, in both sending and receiving countries.

Mass information must be undertaken for two ends: first, to inform potential migrants of migration procedures and constraints and, second, to overcome the negative perceptions that many Europeans have toward increased migratory flows. The latter can be accomplished by conveying the sense that the government is in control and by educating citizens about the benefits to be derived from other cultures—by countering xenophobia and racism (fear) with facts.

In Europe as elsewhere, public perceptions of the migration threat rather than any more objective criteria of absorption capacity determine the extent to which countries pursue more or less liberal asylum policies. For reasons previously outlined, in the public mind the distinction between refugees and migrants has become danger-ously blurred. Exploited by some unscrupulous politicians, this has led to rising levels of xenophobia and racism, including attacks against asylum seekers and refugees in some European countries. Information campaigns must aim primarily at sensitizing the public to minority rights and refugee concerns.

The significant success of public health information campaigns aimed at decreasing smoking or promoting safety belt use high-lights the degree to which ingrained negative behavior can be changed through government-sponsored campaigns. UNHCR's mass information program in Vietnam and most recently in Alba-nia demonstrates how such campaigns in sending countries can help them better manage their migrant outflow.

Under the heading of information, another crucial element is information gathering. Many of the causes and implications of pop-ulation movements are unknown. More research, analysis, and dis-cussion are required if humane and effective strategies are to be formulated. UNHCR as a "frontline" institution does not always have sufficient distance from the problems it encounters daily across the globe to be able to devise imaginative new solutions and strategies. By strengthening our research and analysis capacity, we are trying to change this. UNHCR has established computerized country-of-origin databases and is now strengthening its strategic planning and coordination units. Migration and security, as well as being at the top of the humanitarian and political agendas, must also figure more prominently in the intellectual agendas of univer-sities, think tanks, and other relevant governmental and nongov-ernmental institutions.

The fourth component of the high commissioner's strategy is to link humanitarian activities with peacemaking and peacekeeping efforts. Resolving or preventing the political conflicts that cause ref-ugee flows and/or migration and creating the proper conditions to allow those affected to return home are the most crucial ingredients of any solution-oriented strategy.

In recent years a significant and positive change has occurred in this respect. The essential links between peacemaking, peacekeep-ing, and humanitarian action are increasingly recognized. A fur-ther, and related, change is the renewed confidence in the United Nations as a means of conflict resolution. As a result, the United Nations has launched more peacekeeping operations in the last three years than in the previous 43 years of its history.

Namibia and Cambodia are for the most part success stories. On the other hand, Angola, Bosnia-Herzegovina, and Croatia—and

Somalia, in a different way—illustrate the cost to the international community of acting with too little too late. No action at all, however, would have led to far greater costs in both lives lost and number of refugees. Afghanistan and the Central Asian republics demonstrate the need for sustained government commitment to development and conflict resolution. If it is to bear fruit, such commitment cannot be as fickle as newspaper headlines. Afghanistan, the last major victim of cold war policies, in particular demonstrates the need for prolonged efforts.

The international community, regional organizations, and the United Nations in particular need to become even more active in this respect. Enhanced early warning systems and improved emergency response capabilities need to be linked more closely to the United Nations' political capabilities if the organization is to react faster, more effectively, and with greater cooperation between its humanitarian and political components.

The humanitarian element can contribute to the political process with early warning and emergency response capacities, which free up time and space for démarches, negotiations, and peacemaking efforts. Time and space can prove crucial in saving lives and allowing for preventive diplomacy and thus peace. They permit the slower and more cumbersome peacemaking machinery to begin operating. Over the past 18 months UNHCR has significantly strengthened its early warning and emergency response capacities.

The politicizing of humanitarian causes is surrounded by dangers and opportunities. The very neutrality and impartiality that essentially characterize humanitarian action can be undermined. And humanitarian action can be used as an excuse for political inaction. (The former Yugoslavia is a case in point.) If lasting solutions to the human plight are to be found, however, political problem solving must be more closely linked with added political support for humanitarian action.

The fifth point of the proposed strategy, which is closely related to the previous element, is action against human rights abuses. Mass violations of human rights are a major cause of refugees and displacement.

Articles 9, 13, and 15 of the Universal Declaration of Human Rights expressly provide against exile and guarantee the right to return to one's country of origin. The Nuremberg trials established forced mass exodus as a crime against humanity. Every effort is required to make these concepts more grounded in reality. Governments must be held accountable for the deeds they perpetrate against their citizens.

Provisions against forced exile—the right to freedom of movement and residence within one's own country, as well as the right to return—all imply the right to remain. The concept of the right to remain underlines the basic right of the individual not to be forced into exile—a fundamental human right. Repeatedly, Sadako Ogata has called for more affirmative measures to address those circumstances that force people to flee. The international protection that can be afforded to refugees should not be seen as a substitute for the protection they should have received from their own governments. Preventive measures against such human rights violations become another aspect of solutions to refugee problems. A positive development in this regard is the growing awareness in the international community that states cannot claim national sovereignty as a ploy to prevent "interference" while perpetuating human rights abuses, particularly where other countries carry the burden of refugees and displaced outflows.

In the UN Charter, the notion of sovereignty connotes certain responsibilities for the country concerned toward its citizens. In this respect, it is encouraging to see that repression of national civilian populations is increasingly being perceived not only as a matter of humanitarian concern but also as a threat to international peace and security. Undoubtedly, the security threat caused by internal repression and the risk that it will spill over borders are prompting the Security Council to act in this area.

Peacebuilding and peacemaking efforts require a conceptual framework. The underdogs cannot be helped unless there is a clear conception of who the underdogs are and the most appropriate means to address their concerns. The explosion of conflicts across eastern Europe involving minorities, border setting, and principles of self-determination has demonstrated the inadequacies of our thinking to date on these issues. The international community lacks a consensus, formulated in international law, on such issues as how far the right to self-determination goes and what essential criteria justify a call for statehood. Where opposition groups rail against their government and minorities call for their independence, suppressing other minorities in turn, we are too often at a loss. How do we respond, and how do we know right from wrong? Much thinking is required if the international community's increased readiness to intervene is to occur within an equitable and effective framework.

The sixth element in the strategy, increased activity in the economic and development spheres, is also directed against a root cause of displacement. Through the imposition of sanctions, the negative use of trade as a political tool has become increasingly popular. The challenge is to put trade and other components of the international economy to a positive use in encouraging peace and development.

As mentioned earlier, political factors underlying displacement are closely interlinked with the enormous economic and social challenges facing affected regions, blurring the simple distinction between refugees and migrants. Economic development and aid must be closely linked with the peacemaking and human rights dimensions of a comprehensive approach. Peace must include freedom from war and want. Economic and development initiatives in countries of origin should supplement, not replace, liberal asylum policies in hosting countries.

Adequate resources must be invested in the countries of origin, using a comprehensive, region specific, long-term strategy that embraces trade measures, increased development assistance, and debt relief. Emphasis should be on sustained development with priority being placed on human needs, including job creation, poverty alleviation, education, and health. At present, only 10 percent of overseas development aid from the Organization for Economic Cooperation and Development (OECD) countries goes into these spheres.

The last component in the high commissioner's seven-point strategy is implementing a coherent, coordinated approach. All the previous elements elucidated need to be brought together in a coordinated, coherent manner. The problem of displacement is not peculiar to any one region, nor susceptible to a unilateral solution. By nature, it crosses frontiers. If it is to be tackled in any meaningful fashion, isolationism must be avoided. International cooperation and solidarity must be translated into courageous and tangible action. The various governmental institutions dealing with asylum, migration, human rights, and development need to act in unison within a single, overall strategy. Likewise on the multilateral side, universal and regional organizations such as the International Labor Organization, the International Organization for Migration, UNHCR, the Council of Europe, the Conference on Security and Cooperation in Europe, the European Community, and the OECD have to be brought closer together with their similar and sometimes overlapping concerns. The nongovernmental organizations have an important role to play in the development of any comprehensive response.

The task at hand demands that states look beyond their parochial, national interests just as each institution concerned has to look beyond its organizational interests. We must not allow the myopia, self-interest, and intolerance of the 1980s to determine the future. For both migration and security reasons, the consequences would be disastrous.

Conclusion

The seven-point strategy outlined above contains the essential elements for a European response to the new security issue of migration. Again, these are the seven points: the reaffirmation of protection principles, the adoption of migration policies, dissemination of information, the linking of humanitarian activities with peacebuilding and preventive diplomacy, action on human rights, increased economic and development activities, and the bringing of all these elements together in a coherent, coordinated approach.

In the global, historical context, no region or continent seems immune from the uncertainty and instability that has replaced the predictable universe of cold war relations. Security in this new world is increasingly about coping with nonmilitary challenges. The main threats to security today are underdevelopment, environmental degradation, lack of progress toward democracy, and the movement of peoples. What has become more than apparent is that assistance and political efforts are required far beyond the capacities of charitable institutions to provide them. Refugees, displaced persons, and migrants are no longer simply humanitarian concerns that can be solved by humanitarian action alone.

The central challenge facing us in the post–cold war era is to develop a comprehensive strategy on the movement of peoples that preserves the right of asylum yet makes greater efforts to address the causes of flight—a strategy that allows people to move in freedom and safety without jeopardizing the order and security of our societies. The risks are as abundant as the opportunities. Let us hope Europe does not turn its back on those who are forced to move, but strengthens its long tradition of safeguarding the rights of the oppressed and uprooted. The path that we follow will determine the kind of world we bestow on future generations.

2

At a Crossroads: Europe and Migration

Demetrios G. Papademetriou

Most individuals who migrate do so for one of the following reasons: (1) the host countries' immigration policies (or lack of them) and overall labor needs encourage migration; (2) the North's social, political, and economic rhetoric, as well as its overall commercial propaganda, inspires them to move; and (3) the overriding social, economic, and political conditions at home "force" them to flee.

- The first group will continue to migrate, primarily along legal and illegal channels that the North has created, or simply made possible.

- The second group is likely to continue to increase in importance and will continue to pose a critical policy challenge for the 1990s.

- The third group may pose the truest long-term challenge for the community of nations collectively as the North gropes for durable responses to its causes and for effective mechanisms for addressing its consequences.

In this paper, I focus on issues surrounding the first kind of migrant. Specifically, I examine the conditions in the receiving countries that give rise to and fuel immigration and on the primarily domestic and unilateral responses that offer European countries opportunities to exert more control over migration. The initiatives proposed here are thus rather narrowly focused. It is beyond the scope of this paper to undertake a critical analysis of how conditions in sending societies promote emigration and the crucial long-term initiatives required for solving the migration puzzle (Papademetriou and Martin 1991; Papademetriou 1994).

How Serious Is the Challenge?

An immigration crisis?

Increasing economic interdependence, and possibly an inchoate yet unmistakable sense of a shared destiny, has made the conditions in the South worsen in a number of economic, political, and environmental policy realms. The prospect of disorderly migrations from the South to the North greatly intensifies such concerns. And even if such migration is not yet a first-order concern for many countries of the Organization for Economic Cooperation and Development (OECD), it is increasingly seen to impinge on policy realms that still enjoy a higher priority.

Similarly, although to a much smaller degree, none of the North's errors of social and economic omission or commission (which are discussed in the next section) are *sufficient* conditions to trigger immigration crises there. Nevertheless, they do contribute to a sense of helplessness, even paralysis, regarding the challenge and thus enormously complicate efforts to seize political control of the issue.

The discussion that follows is relevant for *all* OECD countries, although clearly to different degrees. The situation in Europe will be used as the analytical vehicle because it is in western and northern Europe where both contextual and migration-specific explanations seem to have the most direct impact. And it is there that a sense of "things being out of control," if not one of an impending catastrophe, seems to be conspiring with a fundamental uneasiness about the Continent's future prosperity, and an extreme disillusionment with government in general, to generate the most pronounced and organized reactions to immigration.

Western Europe's perception of being in the throes of an extraordinary immigration crisis can be traced to two overarching and mutually reinforcing sets of circumstances. The first is contextual and seems to color everything Europe currently feels and does as it struggles to digest and respond to the enormous changes in the political and social landscape brought about by the end of the cold war. The second is more migration-specific and has two components: East-to-West and South-to-North migration.

The post–cold war environment

The abruptness with which the post–World War II political order collapsed caught the West without a paradigm for policy-making that could help it fully appreciate events in the East. Nor could the West respond with its customary cold war vigilance and coordination. However unsettling, the East-West competition had helped to focus the West's collective mind on a single preeminent threat, while the broader policy of containment allowed governments considerable latitude in matters unrelated to security.

The East's collapse has created a paradigmatic, if not ideological, void in international relations that European foreign policy elites have not yet been able to fill. Their responses appear not only ad hoc and poorly organized but also ineffective. The resulting sense of impotence in shaping, or simply managing, important processes and events has produced a malaise made worse by Europe's pronounced feeling of vulnerability to a myriad of crises—all seemingly intractable.

Although many of these crises affect the South far more directly, they nonetheless reinforce Europe's (and to a lesser extent the North's) anxieties about its own ability to control events and have become fertile ground for political exploitation by opportunists of both the Left and the Right. The harsh social and economic restructuring that global economic integration and interdependence is imposing on all members of the community of nations makes the timing of these anxieties even less favorable by exacerbating individual apprehensions about future economic security.

Three of the most tangible and visible sources of this apprehension have become veritable lightning rods for this Europewide angst: (1) migrants and asylum seekers, (2) the EC–92 process, and (3) trade liberalization negotiations. These processes feed into the intense, anxiety-led introspection taking place in several European societies as they contemplate issues that will fundamentally affect their economic well-being, social cohesion, and cultural and national identities.

Immigration and asylum flows. Two immigration-related issues are especially relevant in this regard. First is the reemergence of large immigration inflows after nearly two decades of essentially steady states in aggregate immigration and "foreign worker" employment totals (see tables 2.1 and 2.2). Continuing interest in and liberalization of family reunification and naturalization requirements—and, in the case of Germany, constitutionally guaranteed *jus sanguinis*–based nationality laws that permit the repatriation of all ethnic Germans regardless of the strength of their claim to German identity—contradict the generally relentless official line that the European countries are not countries of immigration.[1]

These processes have in turn fueled a sense of confusion and betrayal in the mass public as it began to realize that the "workforce immigration" of the previous generation (which a succession of politicians had disingenuously continued to portray as temporary) not only has become "settlement immigration" but may also be the tip of an enormous immigration iceberg.

This sense of vulnerability to immigration is further enhanced by the intensifying incidence of clandestine and otherwise unauthorized immigration. This type of immigration is contributing to a European perception that the prosperous western and northern-central European countries are facing a pincer-like movement.[2] In this regard, both the Mediterranean Sea and the Oder-Neisse River have become Europe's equivalents to the United States' border with Mexico and the Rio Grande, increasingly aggressive efforts at regulation and control notwithstanding.

Another "unwanted" component of these flows, however, seems to be even more important in western Europe's perceived vulnerability. The source of this second "threat" lies with the flows of asylum seekers.

There are two discrete, yet mutually reinforcing, elements to the asylum issue: The increases in the number of those seeking asylum in western Europe,[3] and the related issue of systematic abuses of the asylum system by prospective immigrants who use it as the only available immigration access route to some western European countries.

Aggregate applications for asylum in Europe have increased nearly fivefold since 1980 (see table 2.3). Recent claims for most European countries, however, have either stabilized or fallen in the past few years; in only a few instances have increases been extraordinary. The overwhelming majority of the recent extraordinary (rather than gradual) growth is the result of the war in the former Yugoslavia and the economic and social conditions in certain eastern and southeastern European countries (data not shown; see Papademetriou 1994).

In fact, the gross growth in asylum claims by nationals from outside of the European space has been moderate (Papademetriou 1994). When countries with which specific European countries have had complex "historical" relationships are also isolated in the asylum totals,[4] the remaining absolute growth in recent asylum claims becomes quite modest.

Remarkably, official Europe shows a near disinterest in disaggregating the asylum data and publicly approaching the issue systematically and analytically. This disinterest seriously inhibits

Table 2.1
Absolute and Relative Size of
Foreign Population for Selected Years and Countries
(in thousands and percentages)[a]

Country	1980	1985	1988	1989	1990	1991
Austria	283	271	299	323	413	512
	(3.7)	(3.6)	(3.9)	(4.2)	(5.3)	(6.5)
Belgium	877	846	869	881	904	922
	(8.9)	(8.6)	(8.8)	(8.9)	(9.1)	(9.2)
France[b]	3,714	--	--	--	3,607	--
	(6.8)				(6.4)	
Germany	4,453	4,379	4,489	4,846	5,242	5,882
	(7.2)	(7.2)	(7.3)	(7.7)	(8.2)	(7.3)
Italy	299	423	645	490	781	897
	(0.5)	(0.7)	(1.1)	(0.9)	(1.4)	(1.6)
Netherlands	520	552	624	642	692	733
	(3.7)	(3.8)	(4.2)	(4.3)	(4.6)	(4.8)
Sweden	422	389	421	456	484	494
	(5.1)	(4.6)	(5.0)	(5.3)	(5.6)	(5.7)
Switzerland	893	940	1,006	1,040	1,100	1,163
	(14.1)	(14.5)	(15.2)	(15.6)	(16.3)	(17.1)
United Kingdom[c]	--	1,731	1,821	1,949	1,875	1,791
		(3.1)	(3.2)	(3.4)	(3.3)	(3.2)

Source: SOPEMI, 1993; Eurostat; and individual country reports to SOPEMI.
[a] All 1991 numbers are provisional. Data are rounded to the nearest full number.
[b] France only reports census data; it does not publish interim estimates.
[c] There are no 1980 foreign population data for the United Kingdom.

Europe's ability to regain control of the rhetoric surrounding the issue and to create the political breathing room for devising targeted policies that stand a chance of long-term success.

This is not to say that it is easy to "guide" the issue along the path of rationality suggested here—particularly given Europe's

Table 2.2
Stock of Foreign Labor in
Western Europe for Selected Countries, 1984–1990
(in thousands)[a]

Country	1984	1985	1986	1987	1988	1989	1990
Austria	147	148	155	158	161	178	236
	(4.4)	(4.4)	(4.6)	(4.6)	(4.7)	(5.2)	(6.7)
Belgium[b]	182	180	179	176	179	196	--
	(4.5)	(4.4)	(4.4)	(4.3)	(4.3)	(4.7)	
France	1,658	1,649	1,556	1,525	1,557	1,594	1,624
	(6.9)	(6.9)	(6.5)	(6.3)	(6.4)	(6.5)	(6.6)
Germany	1,855	1,823	1,834	1,865	1,910	1,941	2,025
	(6.5)	(6.3)	(6.3)	(6.3)	(6.4)	(6.5)	(6.7)
Netherlands	169	166	169	176	176	192	200
	(2.9)	(2.8)	(2.8)	(2.7)	(2.6)	(2.8)	(2.9)
Sweden	219	216	215	215	220	237	258
	(4.9)	(4.8)	(4.9)	(4.8)	(4.9)	(5.2)	(5.6)
Switzerland	539	549	567	588	608	632	670
	(16.2)	(16.2)	(16.5)	(16.9)	(17.3)	(17.8)	(18.7)
United Kingdom	744	808	815	815	871	960	933
	(2.7)	(2.9)	(2.9)	(2.9)	(3.1)	(3.4)	(3.3)

Sources: SOPEMI statistics, 1991; individual country reports to SOPEMI; OECD's Labor
Force Statistics, 1992. Comparable data on Italy's foreign labor not available.
[a] Percentage of total labor force in parentheses.
[b] Independent foreign workers are not included. The year 1989 is the last one for which
Belgium has reported foreign labor data.

daily encounter with images of people from the former Yugoslavia
attempting to flee the violence there.[5] Coming as these images do
on the heels of the Albanian refugee crisis, the continuing flow of
asylum seekers from eastern Europe and especially Romania, and
the instability in the republics of the former Soviet Union (with at
least the latter's potential for large-scale outflows)—and reinforced
by almost daily media attention to the issue—the refugee/asylum

Table 2.3
Asylum Applications in Western Europe for
Selected Years and Countries

Country	1980	1985	1986	1987
Austria	9,259	6,700	8,700	11,400
Belgium	2,700	5,300	7,700	6,000
France	18,800	25,800	23,400	24,800
Germany	107,800	73,900	99,700	57,400
Italy	2,450	5,400	6,500	11,000
Netherlands	1,300	5,700	5,900	13,500
Sweden	3,000 [a]	14,500	14,600	18,100
Switzerland	6,100	9,700	8,600	10,900
United Kingdom	4,300	5,500	4,800	5,200
Total	155,709	152,500	179,900	158,300

Sources: Informal consultations, April 1993, and individual country reports to SOPEMI.
[a] This figure is for 1983.

issue serves to further highlight Europe's perceived vulnerability, impotence, and "compassion fatigue."

The EC–92 process. There can be little doubt that the European Single Market idea (integration) still holds the greatest promise for becoming the Continent's "replacement" paradigm. The understandable inward orientation of some key European governments, however, along with Europe's persistent economic problems, has contributed to a loss of confidence and a corresponding loss of momentum in the "integration" of both internal and external EC relations. This notwithstanding the apparent last-minute retreat from repudiating Maastricht, evident both at the Edinburgh summit of December 1992 and at the successful Danish referendum in the spring of 1993.

To be sure, nationalists in several European countries have never been comfortable with the idea of a federal Europe. Aided by a stubborn recession and, in no little measure, by a perception of overreaching on the part of the Delors-led EC Commission, these "Euroskeptics" have succeeded in highlighting the Single Market's implications for certain of the EC members' crucial sovereign prerogatives. Their efforts have not only slowed the pace but, perhaps more significantly, possibly redefined the very character of "inte-

Table 2.3
Continued

1988	1989	1990	1991	1992
15,800	21,900	22,800	27,300	16,238
5,100	8,100	13,000	15,200	17,754
31,600	60,000	56,000	46,500	27,486
103,100	121,000	193,000	256,100	438,191
1,300	2,200	4,700	31,700	2,493
7,500	14,000	21,200	21,600	17,462
19,600	32,000	29,000	27,300	83,188
16,700	24,500	36,000	41,600	18,138
5,100	10,000	30,000	57,700	24,610
205,800	293,700	405,700	525,000	645,560

gration à la Europe," at least for the time being.[6]

The immigration card has also been a favorite vehicle for heightening popular discomfort about further integration. The internal market's free-movement-of-persons provision brought home the reality that Europe's immigration-control policies would only be as good as those of such "faraway" (and decidedly less "disciplined") countries as Greece, Spain, Portugal, and Italy.

Trade liberalization. Whether trade liberalization has taken the form of negotiations under the General Agreement on Tariffs and Trade (GATT), or association agreements with eastern Europe that may eventually include at least Russia, or the intensifying U.S. and Japanese market penetration in key economic sectors, the cold logic of the global economy has heightened the European publics' sensitivities that these processes have apparent "winners" and "losers." Among the latter is agriculture. Although one of Europe's most inefficient and highly protected sectors, agriculture has enormous political muscle and a renowned willingness and capacity to disrupt the social order to get its way.

A somewhat different issue, however, may be making matters worse at this juncture. Some perceive that their governments' room for maneuvering has been severely circumscribed by the fact that competence for many of these decisions has been transferred to the multilateral institutions of Brussels (EC) and Geneva (GATT). These institutions are by definition more internationalist, and they are less susceptible to political pressure. The independence and power of these institutions contribute to an already severe perception of a Europe-wide deficit in accountability and hence legitimacy. This deficit is becoming a force with which European governments will have to come to terms by paying more attention to their publics' real (even if parochial) interests or risking repudiation in the polls.

Migration: East-to-West and South-to-North

The migration-specific issue also has two components. The first, East-to-West migration, is relatively recent, largely hypothetical, and likely to have a relatively short time horizon. It is also an instance where a political "failure" or "near failure" could have potentially large and direct immigration consequences for the West. The second, South-to-North migration, is real, has a much longer time horizon, and will continue to provide a sustained challenge for all European countries.

East-to-West migration.   For nearly three years, Europe's angst about massive, spontaneous East-to-West migration often approached levels of hysteria.[7] What may be most remarkable, however, is not Europe's feeling of vulnerability—which history and geography make understandable—but how in feeling vulnerable the Europeans have ignored some of the fundamental lessons of immigration.

Principal among them is that massive immigration flows are actually gradual processes that build momentum over relatively long periods of time. In fact, if there is one still valid law of migration, it is that immigrants follow in the footsteps of earlier immigrants, taking advantage of familial, village, and ethnic networks that offer them a bundle of "services." These services are essential both to the act of immigration and to successful settlement. They range from financial assistance with migration expenses and the provision of information about and contacts with the host labor market to setting up and maintaining crucial private social and economic safety nets.

Absent such services, flows occur primarily as a result of extreme conditions such as foreign and civil wars, famine, and extraordinary catastrophes. Many of these conditions are predictable—and hence theoretically preventable—and none have so far obtained in the former Soviet Union. Presuming that Europe and the West can recognize and act in their own self-interest, they will not allow the conditions there to deteriorate to the point where uncontrollable flight—rather than emigration--becomes a natural, even an irresistible, option.

This is to say neither that the potential for population movements outside of the former USSR is insignificant nor that the nations of western Europe and the other OECD countries should pay less attention to the events there. In fact, significant—even enormous—population movements are already under way and can be expected to intensify. But they have been and are likely to continue to be primarily internal (i.e., interrepublic),[8] rather than international.[9]

The potential for a spontaneous large-scale East-to-West migration certainly exists and may be much more sensitive to actions by the West than is generally understood. That is not to imply that even the most thoughtful and generous actions by the West toward eastern Europe and the former Soviet Union will obviate emigration from that region. Regular contacts between and among open countries inevitably lead to migration relationships. Some of those stem from little-regulated business relationships; others from formal and quasi-formal (but officially sanctioned) agreements involving "trainees," temporary contract workers, and "worker-tourists"; and still others from regular social and cultural contacts and exchanges, such as tourism and study-abroad programs.

All of these contacts and relationships tend to "leak" into both authorized and unauthorized migration. Some temporary workers are found to be "indispensable" by their employers and are kept on—legally or illegally. Bright and promising students are invited to remain as researchers and faculty members. Tourists are tempted to overstay their visas and seek or continue to participate in the underground economy, and individuals develop relationships with and marry host-country nationals.

All these forms of migration are natural by-products of regular contacts among open societies. Hence, the more the East develops and intensifies its normal contacts with the West, the more significant the population leakage will be. Although it is important for societies to try to control this leakage, it is irresponsible to use the fact of its existence to fan the flames of popular fears about an "invasion" from the East.

South-to-North migration. Although concern about the potential of large-scale East-to-West migration is OECD-wide, its significance seems to vary with a state's proximity to, contacts with, and "openness" toward the former Soviet bloc countries. As a result, although the immediacy and intensity of the concern may be greater in Germany and Austria, virtually every OECD country believes that if things simply got out of control in eastern Europe and the former Soviet Union, the entire North would experience an extraordinary immigration impact.

In contrast to the still largely speculative impact of large-scale East-to-West migration, South-to-North migration is already affecting all OECD countries. Although one specific form of this migration—heavy clandestine immigration—was until recently thought to affect a few OECD countries (particularly the United States), it has now spread throughout the OECD.

Migration from the South has in fact been the principal source of all types of immigrants to the North for nearly 40 years. For instance, most of Europe's "guestworker" visas have gone to nationals of countries that are either formally classified as, or fall (or fell at the time of recruitment) economically in, the "South." This includes Maghrebins, Spaniards, and Portuguese in France, Turks and southeastern Europeans in Germany, and southern Europeans in Switzerland and Sweden (Papademetriou 1994).

Increasingly, all of Europe, including Italy, Spain, and Greece, is under extreme pressure from illegal immigrants from the South. And just as geography makes Germany and Austria feel most directly pressured by and vulnerable to East-to-West flows, so it makes Italy, Spain, and Greece feel most directly threatened by South-to-North flows. However, as the hyperbole about the first wave of migration has come to engulf Europe, so has the reality of the second. This is especially because, in both instances, the proposed elimination of borders among the 12 EC countries and the pending incorporation of most of the European Free Trade Area (EFTA) into that system makes any member state's immigration control "problem" everyone's problem.

Political culture and national identity

Nearly 40 years of immigration and the imperatives of the global economy have imposed a new reality on many of Europe's self-described monocultures:[10] the necessity of making the mutual accommodations that are at the heart of successful multiethnic societies. These accommodations, however tentative and incomplete, have in fact changed the very fabric of these societies. They can also form the basis for Europe's policymakers to maneuver responsibly on the immigration issue and channel its energy productively toward politically and economically rational policies.

Failure to do so will strain these societies further, as the majority culture may try to use its near monopolistic political power to further isolate ethnic, linguistic, and religious minorities. This may lead the latter to adopt their own defensive postures via-à-vis the majority culture. In fact, the greater the intolerance, the more the minorities will feel compelled to "protect" themselves by mirroring the messages of the dominant society's merchants of intolerance and hate. This development gives rise to a siege mentality and leads to behaviors that in turn reinforce the majority culture's expectations that minorities are unassimilable. This conclusion is a recipe for disaster. The longer these conditions go unchecked, the stronger the society's centrifugal forces become, thus making the effort required to arrest and reverse them extraordinary. This is the one area in which statesmanship is most badly needed if European countries are to avoid a social implosion of immense consequences both for themselves and the entire region.

The political culture of many European countries is developing a fundamental fissure. Their political leaders and intellectual elites are becoming strongly "inclusionist" and internationalist. In contrast, the mass public, excited by demagogues and political opportunists and buffeted by an unrelenting economic downturn, is becoming increasingly "exclusionist" and nationalist. Immigration as well as ethnicity, race, and class issues are used as tools to exploit tensions borne of national identities undergoing de facto change. The idea that national identities are inherently dynamic, and thus fundamentally mutable, may be universally accepted in the abstract, or in states where the process of nation building has never really stopped, such as the "new" countries of the Americas and Australia. But, in Europe, it is strongly resisted by most intellectuals and mass publics.

Looking for Causes within Our Own Systems

The economy vs. the polity

Although most migration pressure can perhaps be explained by conditions in the South—the "push" forces that require their own separate analysis (Papademetriou and Martin 1991)—deliberate decisions and nondecisions and their often unintended consequences in the North are also responsible for "pulling" immigrants to advanced industrial societies.[11]

One of the key sources of the North's involvement with and interest in immigration can be traced to economic forces that have sought a competitive advantage in the liberalization of the movement of *all* production factors across state jurisdictions. This development has produced nothing less than a direct challenge to the polity by the economy, a challenge that has placed Europe's sociopolitical fabric under unprecedented strain. Economic forces are threatening to undermine part of the very foundation of the dominant political concept around which the world has organized itself for more than two centuries—that is, sovereign nation-states.[12]

As much by philosophical conviction as by habit, polities are organized along definable social and cultural principles (such as language, religion, and ethnicity) that "bond" societies together and have developed sets of symbols, myths, and ideologies that are by their very nature exclusionist. This exclusionism is most evident in state regulation of the processes and conditions of both access to and membership in the polity—the ultimate expression of sovereignty.

The economy's challenge to these organizing principles is both powerful and direct as it seeks to impose on them its own objectives, logic, and terms of engagement. A polity can resist them and face the economic (and eventually political) consequences of isolation in an increasingly global society. Most polities, however, adapt to them by organizing themselves in ways that allow them to manage and exploit this still evolving reordering.

What complicates this reordering is that, although national authorities have witnessed their power to control events erode under pressure from transnational forces, *no substitute for state power has yet been devised.* Thus the moment may be ripe for giving serious consideration to—and testing—the viability of more supranational avenues. As Kennedy (1993) acknowledges, national governments are still the chief institutions for responding to challenges and managing change; they remain both the building blocks of international institutions and the legitimizing agents of all public international actions. This exacerbates the increasingly fundamental fissure between the polity's rhetoric of independence and the economy's march toward sovereignty-eroding globalization.

The economy, slowly but inexorably, directly and indirectly, challenges traditional political arrangements by gradually removing from the ambit of state control those activities traditionally understood as sovereign prerogatives. Simultaneously, however, citizens seem to turn even more to the polity for "protection" from the economy's internationalist instincts—thus strengthening the polity's stock vis-à-vis the economy and postponing further the resolution of this competition. And as is always the case with fundamental, even epochal, change, there are no political road maps and precious few guideposts for how to manage that process successfully.

The anatomy of dependence on immigrant labor

Dependence on immigrants has usually resulted from the North's economic, social, and political actions and inactions. For instance, management misjudgments that cause firms to become less competitive often lead to demands for government "subsidies."

These subsidies, if granted, may take such forms as price supports, export assistance, special tax exemptions, low interest loans/ loan guarantees, regulatory relief, or direct and indirect assistance with research and development outlays. They may also take the form of government acquiescence to, or even outright "complicity" in, keeping labor costs under control. This may be accomplished through legislation seeking to control improvements in wages and working conditions and/or even prescribe some of the workforce's rights of association. They may also take the form of immigration policies that tolerate or even encourage competition between one's own and foreign workers.[13] The latter is likely to occur in the less regulated, low-wage labor markets in which immigrants, and particularly unauthorized immigrants, concentrate.

Dependence on immigrants may also stem from inattentiveness to the public/private sector partnerships so essential to producing adequate numbers of properly educated and trained workers. According to U.S. Secretary of Labor Robert Reich in a *Wall Street Journal* article, "Why NAFTA Is Good for American Workers" (April 30, 1993), such workers form the very foundation of successful "information age" economies by allowing these economies to compete on the basis of quality, productivity, and innovation. Inadequate supplies of such workers gradually lower productivity, erode the capacity for innovation, and lead to less competitive products (owing to inadequate levels of technological content), subsequent losses in market shares at home and abroad, and economic stagnation.

When persistent human capital deficits coincide with short-sighted public and private sector actions that ignore or devalue incentives for high-productivity, high-wage economic strategies, firms adapt in a number of ways. Some seek and obtain expansive permanent and temporary immigration policies that place few substantive or procedural obstacles to the recruitment of qualified foreign nationals. Virtually all members of the OECD do so, although both the mix between permanent and temporary immigrants and the ease with which the administrative obstacles can be overcome vary enormously.

Other firms make "locational" decisions that allow them to play one production factor off against another, or, in a global economy, one workforce against another. They can do so by locating technical operations in countries where the supply of properly trained workers is both more adequate and cheaper while relocating simple production processes to places where the political environment is stable and predictable, the price of general labor is cheaper, the physical infrastructure adequate to support the operation, and the overall investment and regulatory environments most favorable.[14]

Still other firms, often the least productive and competitive ones, may simply resign themselves to this environment and engage in low-wage, low-skill competitive strategies to remain profitable. Access to low-skill immigrants with little regard to their legal status is an often critical part of these firms' overall survival strategy. This last course, which is becoming a common practice in many OECD countries whether or not they have an established immigration regime, potentially has complex economic, social, and political consequences. The reemergence or expansion of declining or nearly extinct industries (e.g., garments) in several OECD countries testifies to this pattern.

Many OECD countries are already engaged heavily in the process illustrated by the foregoing scenarios. Two additional and more structural sets of circumstances, however, are equally important if that process is to be understood in a fuller context.

Demographic and labor force issues

Most OECD countries find themselves at crucial demographic and labor force crossroads. Following often decades of below-replacement-level fertility, the populations of some OECD countries are aging at rates virtually unseen anywhere until now and threaten to create nearly inverted age pyramids by the end of the next generation (OECD 1989).[15] And as the demographic momentum from earlier periods of higher fertility gradually winds down, these countries face the prospect of sharply smaller cohorts of new entrants to the workforce soon after the turn of the century.

Demography is not destiny.[16] And it is very difficult to focus policymakers' minds on the policy dilemmas that projected labor "shortages" may (or may not) create, especially in the midst of continental unemployment rates unknown for more than a generation.[17] In fact, in most cases neither governments nor the private sector have shown any particular inclination (nor succeeded when they tried) either to rationalize the labor force further or to restructure low-value-added operations and their attendant low-wage labor markets to significant degrees.

Given particularly short shrift are measures for reducing the substantial and increasing segmentation of the OECD economies and labor markets.[18] In its most severe form, segmentation contrasts usually large, highly automated, high-value-added, high-compensation firms offering steady employment with sunset industries and medium- and small-sized firms at the margins of economic viability that offer wages and working conditions increasingly unattractive to the citizens of many OECD countries. To pick up a theme introduced earlier, foreign workers, and especially unauthorized foreign workers, are particularly appealing to these firms precisely because they are much cheaper (often half as expensive as indigenous labor) and "totally" flexible, thus allowing these firms to remain competitive by shedding excess labor in response to demand fluctuations.

In other words, in addition to being cheaper, foreign workers provide marginal firms with a lifeline by being expendable in cultures and legal environments that see stable, long-term employer-employee relationships as the source of both economic viability/stability and social peace. At the same time, however, they create the conditions not only for social and cultural backlashes but also, in a perverse way, for postponing the restructuring decisions that are at the very heart of competitive economies.[19]

To recapitulate, the preponderance of the evidence suggests that economic rationality has been prevailing over not only the polity but also the culture. A point easily missed in the present climate of uncertainty and increasing intolerance, however, is that immigration is not responsible for these changes. Rather, a whole complex of failures in both public and private vision and management has created an environment in which the present perception of a socioeconomic (and increasingly political) crisis flourishes. Immigration, although often featured as a principal cause at the very epicenter, may be at best little more than a sideshow to and a consequence of this larger crisis.

Conclusion: What Might Be Done?

Some observers are naturally daunted by the immensity of the challenges outlined here. Noting the virtual policy paralysis regarding immigration in most European countries in the past few years, they conclude that enhancing controls—even closing the doors—might be the only answer. In my view, "enforcement" (that is, both external controls, such as visa requirements and border controls, and internal controls, such as aggressive programs of interior enforcement of labor and immigration laws) and "regulation" (i.e., a sensible immigration system in place) are not likely to be sufficient answers to the situation described here. They are, however, necessary and as such must be part of the overall response.

Advanced democratic industrial societies cannot engage in measures draconian enough to control situations that have developed their own social and economic logic and structures without doing violence at least to the spirit of their constitutional order and undermining adherence to democratic principles and the rule of law. Moreover, even if one of these societies were to engage in such measures in a fit of nationalism, one must wonder whether these measures could be sustained—both in view of the damage that might be done to the country's standing in the international community, but more important, in view of the possible societal divisions such an effort would generate and fuel once the citizens begin to question the effort's proportionality to the challenge.

According to this essay's thesis, the polity will ultimately be responsive to the economy's constantly increasing pressures to "loosen" migration. Insular policies such as closing borders, aggressively controlling internal labor markets, engaging in the highly intrusive actions (in civil liberties terms) that a serious control effort requires may *not* be viable long-term options.

But if controls provide only part of the answer to the challenge of migration, what might advanced industrial democracies do to manage the issue in a way that enhances the benefits of the process yet controls for some of its most troubling effects? Three broad policy initiatives stand out as having the greatest policy payoff if given sensitive and sustained attention.

Developing coherent immigration policy regimes

An effective immigration policy regime must be consistent with a country's self-perception; conform with its humanitarian obligations; and exhibit clarity of purpose, programmatic transparency and simplicity, and consistency and fairness in implementation. Rather than reaching into the realm of "magic sword" solutions, it must also set modest, and thus attainable goals. Even then, a government must be prepared to tolerate the imperfections and uncertainties that are inherent in every management system.

Such imperfection will be most pronounced in the areas affected by these two factors: controlling clandestine immigration is a goal that eludes all advanced democratic societies, and all immigration systems tend to quickly perpetuate themselves—a quality that begets more immigration.[20]

Self-perpetuation has an economic and a sociopolitical source. The market tends to prefer hard-working immigrants possessing the appropriate skills and attitudes (often associated with lower wage expectations and fewer demands about working conditions) over indigenous workers. The sociopolitical aspect expresses itself in difficult-to-resist demands for family reunification and in locational and mobility choices that create ethnic communities, even enclaves. Concentration allows ethnic communities to gain self-confidence and to organize and seek to influence the further liberalization of immigration policies or practice their own de facto "reunification" outside of the ambit of state control.[21]

European countries no longer have the luxury of deliberating whether to institute regular immigration regimes: de facto regimes are already in place. The formal development of such regimes, in addition to having symbolic value, can provide a pragmatic value in preventing the perversion of a crucial humanitarian institution. Specifically, foreigners' use of the asylum system for obtaining both entry and citizenship has adversely affected public perceptions about the integrity of the asylum system itself.[22]

Even the best-managed and most generous formal immigration regime will not eliminate the dynamic for additional legal and illegal immigration. Absent such a regime, however, both the majority and minority communities will exhibit little interest in integration, reinforcing the mutual animosities between them. But perhaps the biggest advantage of establishing such a regime may come from the opportunity to manage future flows in a manner that allows the receiver to articulate and implement policy priorities that represent its preferences with regard to the timing, size, and composition of the inflows.[23]

The status quo is procedurally disorderly, extremely costly, and socially and politically unmanageable—if not intolerable. It also causes enormous distortions in domestic policies—social, economic, and labor market—that are not directly related; adversely influences many bilateral relationships primarily with principal sending countries; and severely damages one's image in the community of nations. It cannot be sustained.

Managing perceptions about immigration

The caveat against creating unrealistic expectations about immigration policy regimes is this: such regimes need to appreciate up front the importance of managing public perceptions effectively. Such perception management must focus on the key attributes of the policy regime and should target two audiences: first, a country's ethnic communities, and second, the broader public. Many of the individuals who act as information filters in a country's ethnic communities may distort, rather than clarify, matters, which places a premium on consistent actions.[24] The theory in this regard is simple yet compelling: a government's "body language" can communicate messages to its ethnic communities (and, through them, to the potential migrants "back home") much more effectively than any number of policy statements or amount of legislation.

In targeting the second audience—the broader public—the premise should be that an effective immigration policy regime will adopt, articulate, explain, and fairly implement policies that are consistent with a society's ability to accommodate and integrate immigrants. Only by solving the puzzle of managing diversity can European countries turn the "crisis" of immigration into an opportunity. Failure in this regard can render success in all other areas almost irrelevant.

Finally, if Europe is to succeed in managing perceptions about immigration, it must aggressively deny demagogues a monopoly role in shaping the public's mood and must attend to the threat that intolerance poses. No country can afford to have its image tarnished by the irresponsible rhetoric and actions of small bands of opportunists who seek to gain and maintain political advantage by fueling the public's anxieties about immigrants. Most European countries are very closely related; the anxieties of one member should not be allowed to spill over and become the standard to which others must subscribe.

Whether or not European countries have been politically willing to publicly face the issue of immigration, immigration can be a source of human progress both for individuals and nations. Immigrants have been and continue to be an indispensable part of these countries' prosperity. If leaders might lead, they should embrace the issue and engage in the arduous task of reshaping public opinion.

Integration issues

There is no practical alternative to integration. And with few exceptions, no other component of immigration policy is better suited

ɩ for crosscultural learning and for developing common ap-
aches. Legally resident immigrants and nationals should have
ɩ equality across the broadest possible spectrum of social and la-
ɩor market rights—including access to education, language and vo-
ɩational training, employment assistance, and all social rights that
derive from one's right to work. This is a goal to which European
countries can and must subscribe.

In addition to such fully nondiscriminatory treatment, all
longer-term foreign-born residents, which traditional immigration
countries call "permanent residents," "landed immigrants," or just
"immigrants," should be given the option of becoming natural-
ized citizens. Admitting those people to citizenship must be done
through an open and inclusive process with reasonable, transparent, and fair policies. If both policy and process are thoughtfully
integrated, the naturalization effort should have a virtually prede-
termined outcome, particularly if discretion initially errs in the direction of generosity rather than inflexibility and capricious
denials.

Furthermore, those who, for a variety of reasons, choose not to
avail themselves of such a privilege should be given no cause for becoming insecure about their right to stay in the receiving country.
The operative principle in this regard should be straightforward:
with few exceptions (relating primarily to jobs that are truly temporary), one should avoid separating the right to work from that of permanent residence and the eventual rewards and responsibilities of
full political membership. Avoiding the separation of the right to
work from the full social and eventual political participation con-
ferred by citizenship is a hallmark of an open and democratic society.

Finally, more thinking must be devoted to how individuals and
families adjust best to new environments and how best to build a
community by creating a balance between the "rights" and "obligations" on which successful intergroup relations and societal cohesion rest. Appropriate institutions of receiving societies should
work closely with immigrant intermediary organizations to negoti-
ate, adopt, and pursue strategies that produce shared burdens, benefits, duties, responsibilities, and rewards, and that teach a
collective body language imparting the value of mutual accommodation, which is at the heart of successful integration efforts.

This is an extraordinary challenge for multiethnic societies. No
advanced democratic society—from Europe's, Australia's, and, to a
lesser degree, Canada's emphasis on distinctness to the United
States' laissez-faire policies—can legitimately claim to have successfully managed the integration process and untied immigration's Gordian knot.

Notes

1.   As of the beginning of 1993, Germany has modified its approac
through passage of the *Kriegsfolgenbereinigungsgesetz* (the Law to Settle the
Consequences of War), which allows up to 225,000 ethnic Germans (*Aussiedler*)
from eastern Europe and the former Soviet Union to repatriate annually (Papademetriou 1994).

Nearly 1.5 million ethnic Germans have returned to Germany in the
past decade. Sixty percent of them returned in the last three years—397,000,
222,000, and 231,000 respectively in 1990, 1991, and 1992. The origin of these
Germans is increasingly the former Soviet Union, with flows from Poland
(134,000, 40,000, and 18,000) and Romania (111,000, 32,000, and 16,000) having
nearly exhausted themselves during the previous three years. The German
government estimates that between 4 and 5 million ethnic Germans may still
be living outside of Germany (Papademetriou 1994).

2.   "Counting" out-of-status foreigners is always an exercise in frustra-
tion. Most observers would be comfortable with figures placing the number of
unauthorized foreigners in Europe within approximately the same range as in
the United States, i.e., between 2.5 and 4 million persons. It cannot be empha-
sized enough, however, that the existence of a variety of special statuses, such
as that offered to Poles and, increasingly, other East Europeans, by the Germans (three-month "tourist" permits that allow them to work) placed enormous upward pressure on these numbers—although definitional problems
continue to obscure the issue.

3.   Although the consequences of the phenomenon are "shared" by
many countries of both the North and the South, we often lose sight of the fact
that the impact falls primarily on countries in the South. The overwhelming
majority of the approximately 17.5 million refugees and all of the 24 million
"internally displaced" populations remain in the South (see U.S. Committee
for Refugees 1993). These countries are almost invariably the "frontline states"
to the various refugee/asylee–producing crises. Inevitably and increasingly,
however, a very modest but growing, and more visible, spillover of asylum applicants has been finding its way to the North and further fuels its sense of vulnerability to such flows.

4.   Such historical relationships characterize those of Turkey with Germany and Iran, several francophone African countries with France, or the In-
dian subcontinent countries with the United Kingdom. The more important
point to make with regard to these asylum flows, however, is not that they are
insignificant but rather that they probably begin to resemble more and more
immigration flows and that the absence of formal immigration regimes in
many of these countries compels these individuals to try to access the only
available entry route--the asylum system.

5.   Typically, such encounters generate at least two conflicting impulses
in western Europe. The one is of the critical importance that those fleeing
should be provided humanitarian protection and assistance. The other is that
however bad the circumstances, the asylum system is simply overwhelmed
and can no longer respond to the crisis.

6.   This is not unusual in cases where the promise of bold initiatives appears uncertain, and lies in the future, while the fears—manipulated cleverly by opponents to an initiative—loom large and appear to be immediate.

7.   It is interesting to speculate whether the mass publics may have become "fatigued" by, even inured to, the media's—and some politicians'—constant fueling of passions on the issue. After all, mass hysteria can be sustained only for a finite period of time before one becomes anesthetized to the endless catastrophe scenarios—giving way to what might be described as a "crying wolf" syndrome. Whatever the reason, following repeated "predictions" of an imminent "invasion" by "hordes" of Russians, the level of attention to that issue has subsided substantially in recent months—creating at least the potential for a welcome reemergence of reason on this issue.

8.   A most troubling development in this regard is that many of the newly independent republics have been looking "inward" and using their newly found political independence to erect obstacles to the long-term economic security of all "aliens" in their midst (i.e., primarily Russians) by using political power to regain and concentrate all economic advantages in the hands of the dominant nationality. In addition to the elimination of educational enclaves and special privileges, these include such measures as the imposition of linguistic requirements for citizenship and the constriction of political rights.

9.   Some—though probably a very small—share of the 25 million Russians who live outside the territory of the Russian Federation will account for most of those who move. There is very little appreciation in the West of the depth of the processes already at work in this regard even before the Soviet Union's self-destruction—primarily as a result of the "culture of secrecy" that pervades closed societies on matters with at least a putative relationship to internal security.

10.   There is a large element of revisionism and a not insignificant amount of disingenuousness in arguments advanced by some western European intellectuals regarding their countries' purported monocultures. One often has to go only to the first half of this century to find distinctly diverse pasts—along regional, linguistic, religious, and ethnic lines. Immigration indubitably does "stir the social, cultural, and, in some cases, the ethnic/racial pot" and exposes the limits and cracks in the delicate social and political accommodations on which most OECD countries are built. The challenge for Europe is to maintain this spirit of accommodation as it becomes more visibly plural.

11.   A third and frequently overlooked migration force is the social processes which, over time, engage countries of immigrant origin and destination in extremely complex relationships which gradually allow migration to operate almost independently of government actions at either end of the migration flow (Portes and Bach 1985).

12.   This century's two world wars were the apogee of the power of the nation-state system. East-West competition and the cold war extended the "useful life" of nation-states by actually reinforcing the value of protectionism and the search for economic autarky in a fashion similar to that of the interwar period using "blocs" rather than nation-states, as the competing units. The reason is simple: security threats make a state's security function dominant—

often to the exclusion of other functions—and thus reinforce the state's supremacy. Peace, on the other hand, tends to undermine that function's importance (Kennedy 1993).

13. This happens by allowing the market mechanism to choose both its legal and illegal workers. "Tolerating" refers to the only "privatized" immigration regime in existence that ensures the virtually uncontrolled "temporary" (but regularly multiyear) entry of usually high-level managers and technical employees by international business as a necessary concomitant to the globalization of the market—what in the United States is known as the "nonimmigrant" regime. "Encouraging" refers to allowing the same market mechanism to set its demand level (and, in many instances, its price level) for unauthorized foreign workers usually at the lower skill levels.

14. Typically, key measures of such favorable environments include tax and other concessions, weak or nonexisting unions, and labor and environmental protections that are either weak or not enforced.

15. Remarkably, an even larger opening to the East will do little to "correct" these trends as eastern Europe's and Russia's age structures are very similar to western and northern Europe's. Ironically, Germany, one of the OECD countries facing the"bleakest" demographic future, had for a moment discovered a means to delay this process when young East Germans were escaping to the West en masse. With reunification, however, "East Germany" simply reinforced "West Germany's" demographic trends.

16. That is, fertility behavior is influenced by such exogenous forces as economic conditions, the legal regime regarding access to birth control and abortion services, and, to a much lesser degree, government incentives and disincentives. However, historical demography identifies long-term patterns and trends that suggest, for certain countries, such trends have assumed an almost "destiny-like" character (Chesnais 1986).

17. In early 1993, the EC had more than 17 million unemployed workers.

18. One might argue that one policy area which has attained "sacred cow" status throughout the OECD countries—yet one which is inextricably linked to successful structural reform—is that of changes to overall social infrastructure and especially retirement systems. Significant changes in these realms cannot happen without the virtual certainty of enormous social unrest. Yet one must wonder whether subsequent generations of OECD-country citizens will share the same view toward the state's responsibility toward its citizens and will be as timid as the present generation of leaders about reforming the now dominant political formulae for redistributing public wealth.

19. Introducing foreign labor in large numbers can and often does interfere with the serious consideration of other options, such as making much greater and more rational use of female labor and bringing into the labor force such grossly underutilized groups as older workers, minorities, and the handicapped.

20. Most countries with long-established immigration regimes have been handling the demand volume with something akin to "smoke and mirrors." They have either increased the number of available immigration slots (particularly for family members)—a path of least resistance politically—or allowed long queues to form. The former simply avoids confronting a situation to which every immigration system has to face up: that admissions must at some point reach a zero-sum configuration because the demand for visas will always exceed the supply. The latter—formation of queues—creates its own dynamic and builds pressures for more immigration (including the unauthorized reunification of families) and forces our rhetoric about immigration to confront legal and political reality.

21.   The point to glean from these observations is that a country should not enter into regular immigration relationships with unrealistic expectations—rather than that it should avoid entering into such relationships.

22.   The integrity of this critical protection and humanitarian function must be preserved. A direct corollary to such a "putting of one's immigration house in order" is that states who do so may develop the moral courage to engage in two related actions that have been most disturbingly elusive: the removal of unauthorized immigrants and the repatriation of fraudulent asylum claimants.

23.   Developing regular immigration regimes allows a government to choose whom to select and under what circumstances--and, conversely, whom to keep out. As long as the selection criteria are transparent as well as nondiscriminatory (in racial, ethnic, and country-of-origin terms) and are administered efficiently, receiving countries can create for themselves space for policy actions that are not possible in the absence of a formal immigration regime.

24.   Nothing conveys a clearer message abroad than a consistently applied policy.

References

Adepoju, Aderanti. 1991. "Binational Communities and Labor Circulation in Sub-Saharan Africa." Pp. 45–65, in Papademetriou, D.G., and P.L. Martin. *The Unsettled Relationship: Labor Migration and Economic Development*. New York: Greenwood Press.

Chesnais, J.-C. 1986. *La Transition Demographique: Etapes, Formes, Implications Economiques*. Paris: Presse Universitaires de France.

Federal Republic of Germany. *Kriegsfolgenbereinigungsgesetz* (The Law to Settle the Consequences of War). Public document.

Human Development Report, 1992. 1992. New York: Oxford University Press.

Kennedy, Paul M. 1993. *Preparing for the Twenty-first Century*. New York: Random House.

Massey, D., et al. 1987. *Return to Aztlan: The Social Process of International Migration from Western Mexico*. Berkeley and Los Angeles: University of California Press.

Organization for Economic Cooperation Development. 1989. *The Impact of International Migration on Developing Countries*. Ed. R. Appleyard. Paris: OECD Development Center.

Papademetriou, D. G. 1993. "Confronting the Challenge of Transnational Migration: Domestic and International Responses," in *The Changing Course of International Migration*. Paris: OECD.

_____. 1994 (forthcoming). *At the Precipice? Europe and Migration*. Washington, D.C.: Carnegie Endowment for International Peace.

Papademetriou, D. G., and P. L. Martin. 1991. *The Unsettled Relationship: Labor Migration and Economic Development*. New York: Greenwood Press.

Portes, A., and R. L. Bach. 1985. *Latin Journey: Cuban and American Immigrants in United States*. Berkeley and Los Angeles: University of California Press.

Secretariat of the Inter-governmental Consultations on Asylum, Refugee and Migration Policies in Europe, North America, and Australia. April 1993.

SOPEMI. 1992. *Trends in International Migration*. Paris: OECD. Statistical Annex.

SOPEMI. 1993. *Trends in International Migration*. Paris: OECD.

SOPEMI Reports. Annual Country Reports for Austria, Belgium, France, Germany, Italy, Netherlands, Sweden, Switzerland, and the United Kingdom.

The Refugee Council. 1992. *United Kingdom Asylum Statistics, 1982-1992*. London.

U.S. Committee for Refugees. 1993. *1993 World Refugee Survey*. Washington, D.C.: U.S. Committee for Refugees.

3

Shaping a Multilateral Response to Future Migrations

Jonas Widgren

In the current European political context, it is only recently that the relationship between mass movements and political stability has begun to be highlighted. Several factors in combination, however, have increasingly prompted European leaders to warn against the potentials of massive movements of population and their disruptive effects. These include generally increasing South-North and East-West migratory pressures, economic recession, the emergence of extreme-right tendencies, the war in the Balkans, growing political instability in the area of the former USSR, and an expansion of fundamentalism on the southern side of the Mediterranean.

Thus, at the January 1991 Vienna Ministerial Conference on the Movement of Persons from Central and Eastern European Countries, many ministers mentioned in their statements that massive and disorderly movements of people among European states could represent a threat to political stability in all countries concerned. The security dimension of uncontrolled, large-scale migration was further underlined at the Berlin Ministerial Conference on illegal migration, held in November 1991. At the Berlin meeting, ministers stated in a joint communiqué that "uncontrolled movements of people are a destabilizing factor in all countries and place a burden on the harmonious development of relations between European people." At the same time, the ministers responsible for Group of 24 aid to central and eastern Europe, meeting in Brussels, "noted the potential destabilizing effects of uncontrolled migration, and have agreed to take particular account of this issue when developing their assistance programmes."

As a result of the further evolution of political developments in Europe, the interrelationship between massive migratory movements and regional stability has since been discussed at the highest level by the states of the European Community (EC). Thus, in the Declaration on Principles of Governing External Aspects of Migration Policy, adopted by the European Council (meeting at the level of heads of state and governments) in Edinburgh in December

1992, the council noted "pressures on Member States resulting from migratory movements, this being an issue of major concern for Member States, and one which is likely to continue into the next decade." The council further "recognized the danger that uncontrolled migration could be destabilizing." Finally, at the Budapest Ministerial Conference to prevent uncontrolled migration (held in February 1993 and hosting representatives of 36 governments), ministers underlined that "illegal immigration constitutes a threat to public security and stability."

It is clear that European governments are now increasingly prepared to address the migration issue in a general security framework and not only in an economic, social, cultural, humanitarian, or bilateral political context. Yet the multilateral system currently at the disposal of European governments to cope collectively with migration, its causes and consequences, is badly equipped to tackle the expected challenges of tomorrow. The bulk of this multilateral regime was created in the 1950s, under completely different circumstances. Elements of this regime have been much too slow to apprehend changes in the political environment and reluctant to recognize that the immense problems of tomorrow necessitate radically fresh thinking, including much closer informal cooperation with donors as well as with other international agencies. Since the late 1980s, therefore, governments have found it suitable and more efficient to create a parallel and much more flexible, non-institution-based cooperation machinery. The shaping of a new multilateral order to meet the enormous challenges of the future in the migration area, as seen from the European angle, will depend on the possibility of better synchronizing the old and the new parts of the existing multilateral system in the years to come. This is, in a nutshell, the message of this paper.

The paper begins with a short inventory of urgent cooperation needs in this area as seen by European governments, followed by an overview of the parts of the existing multilateral system. It concludes with suggested orientations for the future.

Urgent Cooperation Tasks from the European Perspective

Total annual immigration to West European states, after having acquired rather stable volumes since the mid-1970s when immigration restrictions were introduced all over the region, is now rapidly increasing. More important, the part of total annual immigration that consists of irregular movements is growing significantly.

Whereas in 1985 total immigration to western European states (taken together) could be estimated to be at the level of 1 million, it was about 3 million in 1992. With present trends, the share of irregular inflows as a proportion of total annual inflows will continue to increase from 20 percent in 1985 to 45 percent in 1992 and an expected 50 percent to 60 percent in 1994-1996. Moreover, as the total inflows to western European states have tripled since 1985, it is anticipated that they might well reach the level of 6 to 8 million annually by the end of the decade, without taking into account any possible new refugee emergencies in the eastern part of the region.

Present immigration flows of foreigners to western European states basically consist of five categories (see table 3.1): (1) foreigners who have already acquired the right to enter for residence (preselected workers, family members, foreigners with a right to free EC/Nordic circulation, and preselected humanitarian cases); (2) spontaneous asylum seekers; (3) former Yugoslavs offered temporary protected status (TPS) outside established asylum procedures; (4) "ex-nationals" with constitutional entry right (such as ethnic Germans from Russia arriving in Germany); and (5) illegal entrants (only estimates based on border apprehensions and regularization are possible in this case, per definition). The inflow of the first category has remained quite stable. The second category (i.e., the asylum seekers) is, however, rapidly increasing—from 170,000 in 1985 to nearly 700,000 in 1992, plus 370,000 temporarily protected refugees from the war in the former Yugoslavia who have not been registered as asylum seekers. Most asylum seekers in recent years have been job seekers, not refugees. Of the 2 million asylum seekers arriving in western Europe since the end of the 1980s, as many as 600,000 of them are from central and eastern Europe, pushed out by the economic transition there since the liberation (ex-Yugoslavs having arrived since the war are obviously not included). Large groups of asylum seekers have also come from countries in Asia and Africa for purely economic reasons.

The fourth category (mostly ethnic Germans from all over eastern Europe to Germany as well as ethnic Greeks from the former USSR seeking repatriation, etc.) is currently decreasing as a result of various government measures undertaken to "contain" such minorities in central and eastern Europe. The fifth category, the illegals, is definitely increasing from and via Maghreb over the Mediterranean and via central and eastern Europe to the West. As mentioned above, only rough estimates based on police reporting on apprehended aliens, and on the results of national regularization programs, are possible in this case. Altogether, these trends

Table 3.1
Total Annual Immigration of Aliens to Western European States
(EC and EFTA), 1985–1992

	1985	1986	1987
Regular registered immigration for residence	650,000	720,000	760,000
Constitutional immigration right	50,000	53,000	101,000
Asylum seekers	160,000	190,000	170,000
War refugees from former Yugoslavia	—	—	—
Illegal immigration (estimate)	50,000	65,000	55,000
Total	**910,000**	**1,028,000**	**1,086,000**

Source: Author's compilation of official data.

cannot be expected to decline sharply in the years to come, even with considerable upgrading of border control all over the eastern and the western part of the region and heavy economic transition aid to the Commonwealth of Independent States (CIS) and central and eastern Europe.

These perspectives, combined with the now profound awareness of the potentials of growing long-term migratory pressures on Europe as a result of South-North population and economic imbalances, do indeed cause European governments to worry over the specter of mass movements. In response, they have recently taken a number of initiatives at the international level aimed at addressing the issue of migration pressures in a broader context. Originally, many of these initiatives were not designed for targeting, containing, and attacking migration pressures as such, but rather for establishing the new border system of the EC internal market. The forthcoming abolition of internal borders within the EC necessitated the establishment of a system of joint external borders and the harmonization of visa, entry, and readmission policies. These EC efforts, initiated in 1987, have now gained momentum and increasingly include European Free Trade Association (EFTA) states

Table 3.1
Continued

1988	1989	1990	1991	1992
910,000	1,080,000	980,000	1,020,000	1,240,000
217,000	392,000	417,000	239,000	252,000
220,000	310,000	430,000	550,000	680,000
—	—	—	42,000	370,000
90,000	150,000	210,000	280,000	370,000
1,437,000	1,932,000	2,037,000	2,131,000	2,912,000

(through the establishment of the European Economic Space, or EES, and following the membership applications of Austria, Finland, Norway, and Sweden), as well as to some degree states in central and eastern Europe (notably Hungary, the Czech and Slovak Republics, Poland, and Slovenia).

The harmonization of visa, entry, and readmission policies in every European state configuration is thus currently a primordial task—i.e., between the 9 member states of the Schengen group, the 12 of the EC, the 19 of EC/EFTA, and about 40 of the Vienna and Berlin processes (for a description of these cooperation machineries see the next section). In the framework of these cooperation machineries—all of which belong to the new second part of the multilateral system as indicated above—also short-term bilateral cooperation structures relating to border control cooperation are evolving, in particular with respect to the fight against illegal, crime-related, East-West movements.

As regards the harmonization of asylum policies, an important task for western European governments is to combat abuse of asylum systems through harmonized action and to establish an effective order for the implementation of the country of first asylum principle. EC cooperation on asylum harmonization is now well advanced; the Schengen and Dublin agreements to avoid multiple asylum applications by the same persons may come into force in about one year. Moreover, the "safe country" principle is gradually being introduced, in various forms, all over the area. Thus, applicants originating from what receiving countries have established to be safe (i.e., non-refugee-producing) countries will have an extremely slim chance of obtaining asylum. Another important task is to help upgrade the asylum systems of eastern Europe so that they become compatible with those of the West. Finally, the possibility of "converting" huge government spending from asylum procedures to job creation in sending countries requires increased attention. Since 1985 western European governments have spent nearly U.S.$54 billion on assisting asylum seekers and processing their claims, of which only 15 to 20 percent have been approved. But nearly all applicants somehow manage to stay after their cases have been completely scrutinized. Asylum procedures have thus developed into highly costly and parallel immigration mechanisms. The question is whether government funds, now used in asylum processing, could not be better spent in combating the root causes of these irregular movements.

The intensive work on the new border arrangements of a new Europe, however, has not allowed governments to pay enough attention to the need for developing a comprehensive and multidisciplinary approach (at home and internationally) to ensure that aid, trade, human rights, population, environment, and security policies would increasingly take migration factors into account. Indeed, awareness is now growing at the political level that action in all these areas is complementary and could be better geared toward attacking basic causes of movements and providing alternatives to emigration. There is evidence of such awareness in the 1991 strategy platform of the 16 states participating in the informal consultations and the recent EC summit declaration of external aspects of migration policy. Much too little is being done, however, to further evaluate and elaborate these strategies within national interministerial working groups or internationally in the population policy frameworks of the General Agreement on Tariffs and Trade (GATT), North Atlantic Treaty Organization (NATO), Conference on Security and Cooperation in Europe (CSCE), or United Nations (UN).

Moreover, western European governments are very apprehensive about the constant increase of externally and internally displaced persons in the developing countries and the inevitability of having to invest even more funds and political efforts into alleviating humanitarian emergencies in Africa and Asia through the UN. Discussions are continuing on the mandate of "the blue helmets" (having mushroomed from 10,000 to nearly 80,000 over a couple of years), on the mandate of the United Nations Office of the High Commissioner for Refugees, or UNHCR (now taking care of nearly 20 million refugees and displaced persons as compared with 8 million in 1970), and on what organization should be mandated to protect and provide for the 25 million internally displaced persons. These discussions have deep implications not only for western European states as major donors and UN Security Council actors, but also for the new refugee crisis in Europe and how to handle it.

Europe was not prepared for a new war and a new refugee crisis of its own. Its inability to unite behind a security order that would have choked off the war in the Balkans at an early stage, or to establish a European refugee regime of its own, heavily influences any deliberations on security and migration issues among western European governments. Specifically regarding the refugee issue, western European governments long maintained that Europe should take care of European refugee problems, were they to reappear, whereas UNHCR should deal with the Third World. Yet the global UNHCR agency, largely paid for by the Europeans, is precisely the one supporting the new European refugees.

Many European governments are nevertheless keenly interested in discussing a pan-European refugee regime to be established within an overall European security framework. The discussion on the major features of a security framework to avoid mass movements from taking place are heavily linked to present discussions on the future roles of NATO, Western European Union (WEU), North Atlantic Cooperation Council (NACC), and the CSCE as regional peacekeepers or peacemakers.

To conclude, European governments need a multilateral system that provides an efficient and flexible framework for developing effective cooperation structures, applicable within three to five years, to achieve the following objectives:

- Harmonize visa, entry, border control, and readmission policies among EC states, between the EC and EFTA states, and between them and eastern European states (which would be financially assisted to this end).
- Include a pan-European country-of-first-asylum agreement, joint definitions of safe countries, and the effective return of rejectees to their countries of origin.

- Establish limited programs for organized temporary transfer of labor for employment or training from eastern European to western European states with a view toward creating an alternative to irregular movements.
- Reinforce efforts to ensure free circulation within the EC and EES areas, gradually including nonemigration states in central and eastern Europe.
- Concentrate on forming antiexodus policies in selected countries of origin, including dissemination of accurate information, the strengthening of institutions and migration management capability, enforcement of minority rights and free elections, etc., and development of suitable labor market policies.
- Despite the lack of a comprehensive European approach to the new refugee crisis in Europe following the war in the former Yugoslavia, examine the possibility of establishing a European refugee regime providing temporary protection according to prefixed standards, and including early warning, containment in respective subregions, joint assessment of the need for resettlement, the provision of assistance packages, and implementation of joint return operations when feasible.
- Orient the preventive mechanisms of CSCE, NATO, WEU, and NACC to include population displacements.
- Analyze more effectively the impact of free trade and development aid on job creation.
- Create sustainable nonexodus policies in the developing countries, including population, environment, humanitarian, and human rights policies, in order to create alternatives to emigration.

The Existing Regime and the New Agenda

As indicated above, the existing multilateral regime specifically dealing with migration issues relevant to Europe consists of two parts. The first one has its roots in the 1950s. Since then, it has been represented by well-established institutions whose tasks are to protect migrant workers (International Labor Organization, or ILO) or refugees (UNHCR), provide migration facilities (International Organization for Migration, or IOM), ensure free circulation and study labor market effects of immigration (EC Commission and the Organization for Economic Cooperation and Development, or

OECD), and facilitate the integration of immigrants (EC Commission and Council of Europe). As important as these tasks are and will continue to be, they represent earlier stages of European policy priorities in the migration field. The current overall policy preoccupations of European governments, as described above, relate to the need to forge a joint border area from West to East, possibly with free circulation for nationals; to establish joint long-term objectives for immigration policies; to develop comprehensive development and security strategies to ensure that massive, disorderly and disruptive movements would not occur; and to devise a collective response to refugee movements appearing on European soil.

Most of the discussions, however, both on the various items of the new policy agenda of governments and on how they relate to each other, take place in other forums than those established in the 1950s. Undoubtedly, these are ever more open to adapt their activities toward relevant items on the new agenda. Thus the ILO is increasingly involved in activities relating to job creation in countries of emigration to alleviate emigration pressures. UNHCR is heavily involved, as a lead agency, in coordinating all operations relating to the Yugoslav refugee emergency. The IOM is extremely responsive toward the new migration challenges evolving in eastern Europe and the Commonwealth of Independent States, and, among all the agencies of the 1950s, is the most flexible in adopting its work program to new government requirements. The OECD, the Council of Europe, and the EC Commission all deal with a number of issues on the new agenda but are precluded from addressing those that largely fall into the realm of state sovereignty. Indeed, the cultivation of a comprehensive approach, involving all items on the new government agenda, takes place elsewhere than in or between these specialized agencies.

Generally speaking, there is now an explosion of multilateral efforts to address the new wave of migration. Altogether about 15 multilateral forums deal with the migration problems in Europe, as compared with 5 in the mid-1980s (see table 3.2), and these groups have established a total of 30 to 45 subgroups on various special issues. The groups and subgroups meet about 15 to 20 times a month. During the first half of 1993 alone some 80 to 90 intergovernmental meetings on migration issues were held, involving between 4 and 40 states in the region. This compares with half as many two years ago. About 80 to 85 percent of all these meetings have been held under the auspices of forums pertaining to the second part of the actual networks. A brief description of the first and the second parts of the migration regime follows.

Table 3.2
Multilateral Forums Addressing
Migration Issues in Europe

Forum	Area	Number of meetings in 1993	Number of states participating as members and observers
1. UNHCR Excom and Subcommittee on Protection and special meetings relating to formerYugoslavia	Refugee affairs	8-10	90
2. IOM Council, Executive Committee, and specialized seminars	Migration affairs	4-6	83
3. Intergovernmental consultations (IGC)	Asylum and migration	4-6	16
4. ILO	Employment	2-4	166
5. OECD Working Party on Migration and SOPEMI	Migration affairs	2-3	24
6. Council of Europe			
CAHAR	Refugee affairs	2-3	37
CDMG	Migration affairs	2-3	35
Vienna process	East-West movements	4-5	42
7. EC ministers of immigration and related groups	Asylum and entry control	60-90	12

Table 3.2
Continued

Forum	Area	Number of meetings in 1993	Number of states participating as members and observers
8. Schengen ministers and related groups	Asylum and entry control	10-15	9
9. Nordic coordination group	Asylum and entry control	4-5	5
10. Baltic Sea Council coordination group	Entry control	3-5	11
11. Central European Initiative group	Migration affairs	2-3	7
12. Berlin/Budapest process	Illegal migration	2-3	34
13. ECE	Analysis	3-5	46
14. CSCE process	Prevention	1-2	53
15. ICMPD	Long-term strategies, East-West movements	4-6	(not yet fixed)

Source: Author's compilation.

The first part of the migration regime

The first part of the system actually has its roots already in the reconstruction efforts following World War I. As part of a new international order for peace and security, the International Labor Organization (ILO) was established in Geneva in 1919. The ILO standard-setting and monitoring activities relating to the conditions of foreign labor have developed in a more or less uninterrupted manner in the same tripartite institutional framework since 1919 (composed by governments, employers, and trade unions). The bulk of the ILO migration activities developed in the 1970s were carried out under the auspices of the World Employment Program, geared toward issues relating to job creation in emigration countries. In the 1980s the ILO served as the focal point for the recently completed work on a UN convention on migrant workers. In the early 1990s, in connection with the Gulf crisis, the ILO played a major role in reintegrating dismissed foreign workers into their home countries. In the years to come, ILO intends to concentrate on issues relating to discrimination against foreign workers as well as on possibilities of reducing emigration pressures in specific regions, mainly in the countries of the Maghreb. The ILO has also been active on issues relating to East-West migration and assisted in the preparations for a meeting of European ministers on East-West movements in Prague in 1991.

When the ILO was being established in 1919, a refugee crisis was unfolding in Europe; more than 1 million persons had left Russia, and massive population displacements were also taking place elsewhere. A League of Nations High Commissioner for Refugees (HCR), Fridtjof Nansen, was appointed in 1921. During much of the 1920s close cooperation developed between the ILO and the HCR—the former taking care of all resettlement operations and employment matters relating to refugees. When Nansen died in 1930, a number of organs to deal with refugees in Europe were established to succeed each other. At the beginning of the 1950s the tasks of these institutions—which were then involved in the mass displacement of about 20 million persons by the end of World War II—were taken over by the UNHCR, the United Nations Relief and Works Agency (UNRWA), and the Intergovernmental Committee for European Migration (ICEM, now IOM).

At the time of its creation in 1951 the Office of the United Nations High Commissioner for Refugees was expected to take care temporarily of the residual refugee population in Europe (with a staff of about 30 persons). With the emergence of substantial refugee flows in Asia and Africa in the 1960s, the Third World became the main focus of UNHCR operations. In the second half of the 1980s, UNHCR was thus requested by donor governments to cut back its operations in Europe. But with the mass displacements caused by the war in former Yugoslavia (3.8 million in April 1993), UNHCR activities again expanded significantly in Europe. UNHCR is also developing field activities to meet the assistance and protection needs of refugees and displaced persons in the area of the former USSR. UNHCR's annual expenditures were U.S.$8 million in 1970 as compared with U.S. $1.3 billion today. UNHCR now has a staff of about 3,300 on its payroll.

Parallel to the establishment of UNHCR, the United States took the initiative of creating the ICEM to ensure population transfers from Europe to primarily the United States. (The ICEM inherited 300 staff members of the postwar International Refugee Organization and 12 of its ships.) The traditional role of the organization, now the International Organization for Migration, has evolved considerably beyond handling logistical operations, especially following the changes on the migratory scene in western Europe and the revolutionary developments in eastern Europe. Cooperation with both western and eastern European governments has increased, and its activities have expanded with regard to the return of asylum seekers (under programs in Germany, Belgium, Switzerland, and the Netherlands) and the development of migration policies in eastern and central Europe. The IOM has also launched programs in Albania and Romania, in cooperation with interested states, to disseminate realistic information on migration opportunities and immigration restrictions in western Europe. The organization is actively engaged in the planning of migration programs for a number of eastern and central European countries, as well as for CIS nations. IOM member and observer governments have doubled in recent years. The organization now employs a total of 1,000 persons, of which 150 are at the headquarters in Geneva.

The U.S.–West European postwar deliberations on new institutional arrangements implied a shift of responsibility from the global community to the western European nations themselves in terms of coping with the residual refugee problems in Europe. Hence, one of the first tasks of the Council of Europe (established in 1949) was to create special organs to deal with this. By 1953 the Committee of Ministers of the Council appointed a special representative for national refugees and overpopulation, a kind of European high commissioner with a wide mandate. Moreover, the Council of Europe Resettlement Fund (established in 1956) was to finance related operational activities. The fund (now named the Social Development Fund) has forwarded loans totaling roughly U.S.$10 billion, a considerable share of which has been allocated to migration-related activities (e.g., the present financing of exodus-preventing aid programs in Albania). The Council of Europe is now carrying out a vast array of migration-related activities under its intergovernmental program. Its European Committee on Migration (CDMG) meets twice a year and concentrates on issues relating to the integration of immigrants. Another body, the Committee of Experts on the Legal Aspects of Territorial Asylum, Refugees, and Stateless Persons (CAHAR), also meets twice a year. A number of other related bodies also exist, such as those dealing with bicultural education or dual citizenship. Each third year there is a Council of Europe meeting of immigration ministers; one was held in Luxembourg in September 1991, and one was held in Athens in November 1993.

Some of the Council of Europe's analytical activities in the area of migration and population have much in common with those of the OECD, which mainly are carried out under the auspices of the Working Party on Migration, usually meeting once a year. The migration observation group of OECD, the Continuous Reporting System on Migration (SOPEMI), also meets once a year. The OECD has played a major role as a catalyst for systematic expert deliberations on topical migration issues in a transatlantic context, in particular on the relationship between migration and economic development. A major OECD meeting on this was held in Madrid in March 1993.

Finally, the Commission of the European Communities headquartered in Brussels deals traditionally with a number of items in the migration field, such as the social situation of foreign workers. Because the Treaty of Rome, however, limits the commission's competence to EC nationals' freedom of movement, the commission is not responsible for current EC activities relating to the establishment of the Community's external borders or to the harmonization of the EC states' asylum and immigration policies. Instead, this cooperation is carried out under a special intergovernmental umbrella (see below). The European Council of Maastricht in December 1991 confirmed this division of responsibilities and decided that visa policies alone were covered by full Community competence. However, the Commission has been granted certain co-initiative powers with the member states. It should also be mentioned that all EC cooperation on these issues is monitored by a group called the National Coordinators on the Freedom of Move-

ment of Persons, which is responsible for ensuring that the precon-
ditions for abolishing of internal frontier controls, as defined in the
Palma document of June 1989, are implemented in time. In this
structure, the commission participates in its full capacity.

The second part of the migration regime

By the mid-1980s, when irregular migratory flows in Europe first
emerged, the above-mentioned multilateral institutional machineries were at the disposal of European governments, had they wished
to intensify multilateral cooperation. For a number of reasons, however, they did not opt for an overhaul of the existing regime. Rather,
they opted for a cautious trial-and-error creation of a parallel intergovernmental regime, more forceful and flexible with respect to the
rapidly changing migration picture and to the expected challenges
of the future, and closer to the European capitals. Essentially, European governments decided that they had, first, to define among
themselves their own new objectives vis-à-vis migration before for-
malizing new tasks to be entrusted to the existing regime, taking
into account that controlling migration is by definition an act of
sovereignty. To a very large extent, ministries in capitals execute the
secretariat functions for all these new collective intergovernmental
processes, assisted by small joint clearinghouses or coordination
groups. The main elements of this second new part of the regime
follow.

The most important element is undoubtedly the intergovernmental cooperation machinery established by the EC Ministers of
Immigration in 1987. The ministers gather at least twice a year. The
state that is presiding over the Community also holds the presi-
dency. The ministers are assisted by a group of senior officials, the
so-called Ad Hoc Immigration Group (whose activities are prepared by various subgroups on asylum, external frontiers, forged
documents, admission/removal, information exchange, etc.). The
Secretariat General of the Council of Ministers in Brussels serves
these groups, in close cooperation with ministries in the capitals.
Two conventions have been prepared, the Dublin Convention of
1990, "Determining the State Responsible for Examining Applications for Asylum Lodged in One of the Member States of the EC" (a
draft convention parallel to the Dublin Convention has been forwarded to certain EFTA states), and a second convention, called the
"Crossing of External Frontiers of Member States" (a bilateral problem between the U.K. and Spain regarding the status of Gibraltar is
holding up the signature). The Maastricht decisions have greatly

reinforced EC intergovernmental cooperation on asylum and immigration issues. An EC center for "information discussion and exchange on asylum" (CIREA) has been established and a similar center for border control and immigration issues is being put together within the EC Council structure. Finally, a special subgroup on refugees from the former Yugoslavia has been established. Altogether, the relevant EC groups had a total of about 50 meetings during the first half of 1993 only.

An exercise that parallels the work of all the EC states on asylum and border control issues, but which is more elaborate, is carried out between the signatories of the 1985 Schengen Accord on the abolition of internal borders (the Schengen Group). The original signatories of the agreement (Belgium, France, Germany, Luxembourg, and the Netherlands) adopted in Schengen, Luxembourg, in December 1989, a special agreement on country-of-first-asylum that basically corresponds to the Dublin Convention. Italy joined the group in 1990, Spain and Portugal followed in 1991, and in 1992 Greece became a member. The chairmanship of the Schengen Group rotates among the member states. In March 1991 the Schengen states concluded an agreement with Poland on the readmission to Poland of persons having arrived irregularly to the Schengen states from Poland.

Another multilateral arrangement, the Berlin process, emanates from discussions within the Vienna Club, a forum established in 1978 for security cooperation among the ministers of interior and justice of Austria, France, Germany, Italy, and Switzerland. The Vienna Club has recently stepped up discussions about cooperating on border control issues as they relate to asylum and migration. In principle, the group meets every second year. The German government invited all member states of the club and the EC, as well as the 13 eastern and central European states, to a Ministerial Conference in Berlin in October 1991 to discuss "measures for checking illegal immigration from and through Central and Eastern Europe." A group under the chairmanship of Austria, and including Hungary and Italy, became responsible for further action in the framework of what was named the Berlin process. This process, involving about 36 states in Europe, resulted in the February 1993 Budapest Ministerial Conference on uncontrolled migration. The conference adopted recommendations covering all issues relevant to increased cooperation on border control in Europe in an East-West context. Moreover, Austria proposed at the conference a European migration convention, and Germany suggested a burden-sharing scheme for return operations. Hungary is chairing the steering group for what now is called the Budapest process. The Vienna process on East-West movements originated at the Ministerial Conference on the Movement of Persons from Central and Eastern European Countries, which was held in Vienna in January 1991 at the invitation of the government of Austria under the auspices of the Council of Europe. The conference brought together 35 states. Working groups on visa harmonization (chaired by France), on the establishment of a special institution for information exchange (chaired by Hungary), and on new solidarity structures between states (chaired by Italy) are involved in follow-up activities. The latter working group has prepared a major report entitled "Collective European Cooperation with Respect to the Movements of People." This report also covers issues discussed in the context of the Berlin/Budapest process. Austria is chairing the steering group for the Vienna process.

The Intergovernmental Consultations on Asylum, Refugee, and Migration Policies in Europe, North America, and Australia, often referred to as the informal consultations (IGC), were originally conceived as a forum for information exchange between UNHCR and like-minded OECD governments. These consultations, initiated in 1985, developed between 1989 and 1992 into an important regional multilateral mechanism involving 16 governments. Nearly 100 meetings were held in the IGC framework between 1985 and 1992. Since 1993, however, the Geneva-based secretariat for the consultations has again become more closely linked to UNHCR through a special hosting arrangement in which IOM technically participates.

To serve the Vienna and the Berlin/Budapest processes and to develop long-term migration strategies in a broader security context, the governments of Austria and Switzerland established in the summer of 1993 the International Center for Migration Policy Development (ICMPD), located in Vienna. Other governments in western and eastern Europe have been invited to join ICMPD on an equal basis. The Center will operate as a multilateral clearinghouse well adapted to the new migration cooperation needs, in particular with respect to central and eastern Europe.

Finally, following a U.S. initiative, the CSCE has now started activities in the migration field, beginning with a seminar in Warsaw in April 1993. Moreover, a number of European subregional intergovernmental forums deal specifically with asylum and migration issues, such as the special Nordic Joint Advisory Group, established in 1987, and the Working Group on Migration of the Central European Initiative (previously the Hexagonale), which since the spring of 1992 has consisted of Austria, Croatia, the former Czech-

Slovak Federal Republic (CSFR), Hungary, Italy, Poland, and Slovenia. The group was established in 1990. A Baltic Sea Council migration group involving 13 governments was established in 1993.

What unites all these processes (EC cooperation, the Schengen Group, the Berlin/Budapest and Vienna processes, the informal consultations, and ICMPD) is their regional grouping of governments in a goal-oriented collective approach. The foundation has undoubtedly been laid by Schengen and the Twelve, for a certain time complemented by the informal consultations, pending the entry of most EFTA states in the EC. This, in turn, has been complemented by the Vienna and Berlin/Budapest processes and most lately by ICMPD. The question now is how to gear all these processes—better synchronizing the first with the second part of the system—toward creating a new multilateral order that would prevent mass movements from becoming a security threat in Europe.

Toward a New Multilateral Order

Achieving a new multilateral order is obviously related to overall global challenges as well as the necessary transformation of the whole international system to cope with mass movements. The discussion on the requirements of the global regime is as scattered and uncomprehensive as the one relating to the European regime. At the global level, the UN secretary general's Agenda for Peace, the discussions of the Independent Commission on Global Governance, the hammering out of the role of the UN coordinator for humanitarian affairs vis-à-vis the one of UNHCR, the development of cooperation between UNHCR and IOM, the recent interest in migration issues on behalf of the UN Development Program (UNDP) and the World Bank, the deliberations of the UN Commission on Human Rights on the need for an organ to take care of the internally displaced, and the preparations of the 1994 UN Population Conference form some illustrative but scattered elements. But a comprehensive approach is lacking, as well as discussions on the establishment of a focal point to elaborate such a global approach.

At the European level, there is at least a new set of proclaimed objectives, forming a comprehensive whole, notably the recent Edinburgh declaration on external aspects of migration policy. But where is the master plan for implementation and operations? More or less, all organs now have migration on their agenda, from NATO and CSCE to the Group of 24 and the ECE (UN Economic Commission for Europe). This is in addition to the specialized organs and processes enumerated above. The input for such a cooperation blueprint on the security aspects of European migration—that is, better synchronizing the operations of all actors at the multilateral level—can come *only* from capitals acting forcefully in concert, not from the system as such. And it must probably come mainly from committed governments acting through the Brussels network (EC presidency/EC Council, Group of 24, and NATO/NACC) and the Vienna network (CSCE, Vienna, Berlin/Budapest, and ICMPD processes), rather than from the Geneva network, influenced as it is basically by humanitarian aspects. Such concerted action to form a new, sustainable, streamlined, and efficient regime must start now, lest this task become even more cumbersome.

4

Involuntary Migration: Refugees in the New Europe

Kathleen Newland

Mass flows of refugees are a feature of the new Europe anticipated by few observers. More than 30 years after the last of its post–World War II refugee camps were closed, Europe is again confronted with a massive refugee emergency originating in the former Yugoslavia. Moreover, the number of individuals from all over the world seeking asylum in European countries each year has risen nearly 20-fold since the 1970s, although the distribution among countries is very uneven. The security dimensions of the phenomenon for both sending and receiving countries are extremely complex.

In the European context, four elements set the stage for the discussion of policy toward refugees. One is the tragedy that has unfolded in the former Yugoslavia. The second is the dreaded prospect of mass flows of refugees from the former Soviet bloc, as the heavy-handed stability of Communist rule has given way to bitter power struggles often defined along ethnic or national lines. The third is the process of European integration, which has lent urgency to the tasks of developing common immigration and border policies. Fourth is the asylum crisis in western Europe, in which a loss of public and official confidence in asylum procedures is complicating the response to refugee emergencies.

Against this background, a far-reaching change of perspective on refugee policy is taking place in western Europe, as in other industrial countries. The shift is far from complete, and there is much inconsistency and incoherence in current policies. Although many states have taken unilateral action to change—usually to tighten—their asylum laws and practices, a great deal of discussion, and some action, is also taking place on how to deal collectively with problems of involuntary population movements. This renewed emphasis on multilateral cooperation to address mass displacement springs in part from the perceived need to complete the transition to a coherent policy suited to present-day realities.

What are these realities? One is the enormous growth in the numbers of displaced people worldwide—more than 18 million men, women, and children are refugees, and roughly 24 million are internally displaced.[1] Europe hosts only a small fraction of the world's refugees, most of whom find sanctuary in neighboring Third World countries. But the upsurge in asylum seekers since the late 1980s, and the great difficulties that European states have in expediting their claims, seems to have given many Europeans the sense of a system out of control.

Most of today's involuntary migrations take place in the context of armed conflict, and many individuals who arrive spontaneously to claim asylum in Europe come from war-torn countries such as Iraq, Sri Lanka, and Somalia—and of course from the former Yugoslavia. The most widely accepted legal definition of a refugee, found in the 1951 Convention relating to the Status of Refugees, makes no specific provision for individuals fleeing from violence and chaos in their own countries.[2] Nor have European governments developed a firm consensus on the treatment of war refugees. They have supported the recognition of such people as full-fledged refugees under regional arrangements in, for example, Africa and Central America, and have given them aid out of their humanitarian budgets through the office of the United Nations High Commissioner for Refugees (UNHCR) and other organizations. But there is considerable resistance to large-scale arrivals directly into Europe itself, where the increased numbers of asylum seekers from eastern Europe and developing countries have exacerbated racial and cultural tensions already heightened by the labor migration of the 1960s.

A third new reality is that the refugee flows are increasingly commingled with economically motivated migrants and others with no valid claim to international protection under asylum provisions. The perception is widespread that the asylum system is being abused by those who leave their own countries to seek economic advancement rather than to escape persecution—and the perception is doubtless justified in many instances. As western European states have narrowed—and in many cases virtually closed down—the channels for regular labor immigration, the asylum system offers one of the few opportunities for entry. Public resentment at the misuse of asylum channels is aggravated by the coincident economic stagnation in western Europe, which has seen unemployment rise to more than 17 million people—nearly 12 percent of the population.

Finally, the background to refugee policy in Europe (and other regions) has been changed dramatically by the end of the cold war. Western states used to offer asylum almost without question to individuals who emigrated from communist countries.[3] Exit restrictions limited the outflows, but those who managed to reach the West were generally accepted without much inquiry into their motivations. Ironically, the same regime changes in central and eastern Europe and the former Soviet Union that lifted exit restrictions also weakened the assumption that those who left were in danger of persecution. The bulk of the increase in asylum seekers in western Europe since the late 1980s, particularly in Germany, have come from the East. For the most part, however, the governments of the source countries are willing to engage in dialogue with the receiving countries and to work with them to develop humane ways of dealing with asylum seekers who prove not to qualify for refugee status.

European Preoccupations

The disintegration of Yugoslavia and the subsequent wars among the successor states have once again brought mass outflows of refugees to Europe. More than 700,000 persons have become refugees outside the states that once made up Yugoslavia. More than 4 million of those who remain are displaced or under siege. The dimensions of the crisis dwarf the flows from Hungary in 1956 (about 200,000 people) or Czechoslovakia in 1969 (about 80,000).

Western European states have been actively involved in the Yugoslav crisis, with the European Community (EC) sponsoring peace negotiations together with the United Nations (UN), and both the EC and individual states making major contributions to the expenses of the humanitarian relief operation spearheaded by UNHCR. The bulk of the UNPROFOR peacekeeping troops are European. On the treatment of refugees, however, the policies of the European states vary widely. Some have been extremely generous in providing some form of asylum to war refugees: Germany has taken in 220,000 refugees from the former Yugoslavia, Austria about 73,000, and Switzerland some 70,000. This contrasts with France and the United Kingdom, which have admitted 5,000 or fewer. The uneven burden sharing in this dimension inevitably causes some tensions among the allies (although Britain and France argue that their commitment of ground troops should be weighed in the same balance as refugee admissions).

There is no question but that most of those who have fled their homes in the former Yugoslavia fit the refugee definition of the 1951 Convention, facing persecution on grounds of both nationality and religion. Yet the numbers are overwhelming the conventional asylum system, which assumed that anyone found to be a refugee would resettle permanently in the country of asylum. There are both practical and philosophical reasons to resist this solution for the refugees from former Yugoslavia. One is the absorptive capacity of the receiving countries, which feel, rightly or wrongly, that their societies and economies cannot or will not absorb the numbers of people who are at risk of becoming refugees. More compelling, though sometimes also self-serving, is the argument that it is wrong to acquiesce in the expulsion of whole populations from broad swaths of territory in Croatia and Bosnia and Herzegovina. Rather than resettle the refugees for good, the international community must insist on a political settlement that allows them to go home.

A number of European countries have developed provisions for temporary asylum in response to the needs of people fleeing the war and the campaigns of expulsion in former Yugoslavia. Although the content and procedures vary from country to country, in general they suspend normal refugee-determination procedures and simply allow people to remain until conditions stabilize in their own country.[4] But as prospects recede for a negotiated settlement that permits repatriation, western Europe's dilemma grows as it faces the possibility of having to absorb additional hundreds of thousands of refugees from former Yugoslavia.

The preoccupation with Yugoslavia is intensified by the fear that the Balkan conflict may be only the first of a series of ethnonationalistic conflagrations to come elsewhere in eastern Europe and the former Soviet Union. At the time of the breakup of the USSR, something close to panic ensued in western Europe as the specter loomed of millions of former Soviet citizens heading west to escape political and economic chaos. Although western Europe has indeed seen a sharp rise in asylum seekers from the eastern and central European states, the outpourings from the republics of the former Soviet Union have thus far not materialized. Displacement--and its scale is considerable—has largely been contained within the territory of the former Soviet Union. The entire Azeri population of Armenia has fled, but mostly to Azerbaijan or adjacent areas of Turkey and Iran; about 300,000 Armenians who used to live in Azerbaijan have moved to Armenia or to Russia. Approximately 100,000 South Ossetians have fled from Georgia into the Russian autonomous republic of North Ossetia. Meskehtian Turks forced to leave Uzbekistan have ended up in Azerbaijan and Russia. A great many ethnic Russians resident in other republics have quietly relocated to Russia. The potential for further displacement is vast. One estimate is that as many as 65 million people were residing outside the areas of their ethnic origin at the time the Soviet Union ceased to exist.[5] Political instability and economic decline give little comfort to European officials still anxious about the possibility of refugee flows from the region.

This anxiety has prompted European states to form ad hoc groups to share information and coordinate policies on population movements originating in eastern Europe and the former Soviet Union as well as in other parts of the world (see chapter 3). The impetus to do so has gained momentum from the process of European integration, which has as one of its goals the free movement of people among the EC member states. In July 1993, nine of the EC member states agreed to abolish formal passport controls for people traveling among the nine by the end of the year, but made the measure conditional on improvements in controls on people coming from outside the group.[6] The agreement, known as the Schengen Accord, also foresees the creation of an information system linking police and immigration authorities in the participating states. The harmonization of asylum procedures and practices is an important element of the system. Without it, the country with the least stringent requirements could be expected to serve as a port of entry to all nine countries for people who would not have been admitted directly to the others.

Confidence in the asylum system is low throughout western Europe, both from those who find it too lax and those who fear it is becoming too restrictive. In virtually every country, it is a contentious political issue. The procedures for hearing and judging asylum cases are slow, cumbersome, and extremely expensive. It is estimated that European countries spend as much as 7 billion dollars a year—a figure several times the size of the global budget of UNHCR—on adjudicating claims and supporting applicants while their cases are pending. Huge backlogs of cases have accumulated, and the judgments eventually rendered often seem to be inconclusive in practical terms, with many of those who are determined not to be refugees allowed to stay nonetheless. In Britain, for example, in 1992, only 6 percent of the asylum cases heard resulted in positive decisions and only 20 percent were negative. The vast majority—74 percent—were neither, but received exceptional leave to remain.[7]

Most European governments find it difficult to deport asylum seekers whose cases are rejected. Groups of asylum seekers often have strong advocates in the asylum countries, who for political or humanitarian reasons vocally oppose deportation. Many politicians and members of the public are uncomfortable with the thought of sending people home to situations of misery and chaos, even if they are not in danger of persecution. The determination procedures meant to distinguish between refugees and nonrefugees are not foolproof and often seem to be arbitrary in their judgments. All of these factors, combined with the great time and expense involved in adjudication, compound the impression that the asylum system is not functioning as intended.

A number of governments have recently taken steps to tighten asylum laws, including Austria, Germany, the Netherlands, Spain, and the United Kingdom. Others have begun to interpret more narrowly the grounds on which asylum is granted or to require very high standards of proof that an individual does have a well-founded fear of persecution. Still others have restricted the mobility, welfare support, or work privileges of asylum seekers awaiting adjudication of their claims. More positively, determination procedures are being rationalized so that well-founded cases can be more quickly and easily distinguished from unfounded ones.

European governments have adopted a range of tough measures aimed at deflecting illegal immigration. The measures include visa requirements, often aimed at countries afflicted by civil strife, and sanctions against transport companies that permit people to travel without proper entry documentation for their destinations. In 1991 alone Britain issued 9,521 airline fines on these grounds. Although designed primarily to keep out economic migrants, such measures are likely to be equally effective against refugees.

Given the difficulty and expense of asylum procedures and the trouble involved in deportations, governments would prefer to minimize direct applications. The obligation to accept as a refugee anyone who manages to enter a state's territory and conforms to the definition contained in the 1951 Convention is more or less intact, but it is increasingly hedged by what James Hathaway has called the "emerging politics of non-entree."[8] The visa requirements, carrier sanctions, strengthening of border defenses, and interdiction before entry into the country of asylum are all measures that constrain entry into normal asylum procedures.

To give just one example of the somewhat surreal quality of some of these barriers to entry, Britain in late 1992 imposed visa requirements on nationals of Bosnia and Herzegovina requiring travelers to obtain a visa before visiting Britain—but the United Kingdom has no consulate in Bosnia and Herzegovina. A Bosnian may obtain one only by stopping in a third country en route. But asylum applications are not accepted from anyone who has stopped in a third country, where it is presumed that he or she could have applied for protection. So the regulations make it virtually impossible for a Bosnian to seek asylum in Britain.[9]

The new emphasis on denying entry to people without proper travel documents, although a reasonable way to deal with illegal immigration, hits refugees hard. People fleeing from persecution in their own countries, particularly at the hands of the authorities, are the least likely to have proper documents. Safeguards to ensure that people who genuinely need protection can slip past the restrictions do not, thus far, inspire confidence. The adoption of exclusionary policies in one country tends to deflect flows to neighboring countries, thereby putting pressure on them to fall into line. Thus, for example, virtually all European states have now adopted visa requirements for Bosnians.

The 1951 Convention relating to the status of refugees, to which virtually all the European states are signatories, provides that "signatories shall not impose penalties, on account of their illegal entry or presence, on refugees who, coming directly from a territory where their life or freedom was threatened . . . enter or are present in their territory without authorization."[10] The politics of nonentree amounts to a competitive scramble among European (and other) states to ensure that refugees do not arrive directly into their territory.

The dimensions of the European asylum problem need to be put in perspective. The intense and often emotionally charged debate gives the impression that the fears of being overwhelmed by asylum seekers are out of proportion to reality (see table 4.1). In most cases the annual totals of asylum applications have increased significantly since the early 1980s. But only in Germany and Sweden are the numbers at all large in relation to population and still on a sharp upward trend. (The ratios of asylum seekers to population were 0.56 percent and 0.94 percent, respectively.) As Germany revised its asylum law in 1993 and Sweden reduced benefits to asylum seekers, the direction of these trends may soon reverse. In France and Britain the number of claims in 1992 amounted to less than 0.05 percent of population. In every country only a small proportion of the applicants were likely to be given refugee status.

Moreover, asylum applications have actually gone down from their historic highs in the late 1980s and early 1990s. Far from being out of control, the stream of asylum applications has diminished, in some cases quite sharply, as measures of control have been adopted. What worries many refugee institutions and individuals who work with refugees is that in the exercise of their sovereign

Table 4.1
Number of Asylum Seekers in
Selected European Countries, 1983–1992
(in thousands)

Country	1983	1984	1985	1986	1987	1988	1989	1990	1991	1992
Germany	19.7	35.3	73.9	99.7	57.4	103.1	121.3	193.1	256.1	438.2
Sweden	3.0	12.0	14.5	14.6	18.1	19.6	30.4	29.4	27.4	83.2
Denmark	0.8	4.3	8.7	9.3	2.8	4.7	4.6	5.3	4.6	13.9
Spain	1.4	1.1	2.4	2.3	2.5	3.3	2.9	6.9	7.3	12.7
Belgium	2.9	3.7	5.3	7.7	6.0	5.1	6.1	13.0	15.2	17.7
France[a]	15.0	16.0	25.8	23.5	24.9	31.7	58.8	49.8	45.9	26.8
Switzerland	7.9	7.5	9.7	8.6	10.9	16.8	24.4	35.9	41.7	18.2
Austria	5.9	7.2	6.7	8.7	11.4	15.8	21.9	22.8	27.3	16.3
United Kingdom[b]	4.3	3.9	5.5	4.8	5.2	5.3	15.6	25.3	44.8	24.6
Netherlands	2.0	2.6	5.7	5.9	13.5	7.5	13.9	21.2	21.6	17.5

Source: UNHCR, *The State of the World's Refugees 1993* (New York: Penguin, 1993).
[a] The 1992 figure includes refugees resettled under French resettlement quota.
[b] The figure for 1992 refers to asylum applications ("cases") only. The figures for 1989–1992 are estimates.

right to control their borders, many states in Europe and elsewhere are narrowing the options for escape from violence and persecution. The search for alternatives has thus turned the spotlight of refugee policy toward prevention.

A European Refugee Strategy

The increasing pressures on the European asylum system reflect the turmoil of a world from which western Europe cannot hope to insulate itself. The war in the former Yugoslavia and the growth in asylum applications from elsewhere in the world have shown that the refugee problem is not a distant humanitarian concern but a threat to domestic tranquility and security. Thus far, the most coherent responses have been defensive ones, which focus too narrowly on the asylum system in Europe. UN High Commissioner for Refugees Sadako Ogata has urged European states and societies to take a broader and more outward-looking approach to refugee and asylum policy.[11] In doing so, Europeans have much to learn from other parts of the world, where far poorer countries with proportionately far larger refugee populations have taken part in innovative regional strategies that address the needs of both sending and receiving countries as well as the refugees themselves. The International Conference for Refugees and Exiles in Central America, known by its Spanish acronym CIREFCA, and the UN Transitional Authority in Cambodia are two examples of programs that integrate humanitarian and political strategies, including the voluntary repatriation of refugees.

The high commissioner suggested that a comprehensive European refugee strategy should contain five elements. The first and most fundamental is liberal application of the 1951 Convention to protect those who are in danger of persecution from being returned to danger. The second element is maintenance of a clear distinction between economic migrants fleeing poverty and refugees fleeing persecution and violence. Both groups may need and deserve assistance, but their needs differ, as do the obligations that states have toward them. Neither the interests of states nor the interests of refugees are served by blurring the categories. Greater assistance to refugee programs in poorer parts of the world is the third element of the strategy. It helps promote solutions in the countries of origin and helps developing countries that receive refugees continue to provide asylum. The fourth element involves serious efforts in prevention, focused on promoting human rights and sustainable development in refugee-producing countries. Finally, public information is an important part of a comprehensive strategy. Migrants often leave their homes without either a clear understanding of the grounds on which they can legitimately claim asylum or an accurate picture of the likely consequences of a move. Information can correct misapprehensions and steer people toward the most appropriate channels for their circumstances. Public education is also necessary to combat xenophobia and to inform the European public about the plight of refugees.

Although each of the five components can be found in the policies of individual European governments, they would have far more impact if they were knit together in a coherent regional response that addressed the causes as well as the consequences of people being forced to flee. Of course, this is not a task for Europe alone. Regional policies need to fit within a broader multilateral effort to deal humanely with involuntary migration.

New Directions in Refugee Policy

The end of the cold war signified the end of political paralysis in multilateral institutions. East-West polarization made it virtually impossible to bring multilateral pressure to bear on the countries from which refugees originate. A cooperative evolution, even revolution—of a sort not possible in the previous four decades—is now under way in policies on mass exodus.

The shift in multilateral response to mass displacement may be characterized in the simplest possible terms as a shift in emphasis away from asylum and resettlement toward prevention and repatriation. Some aspects of the shift, particularly the more restrictive attitudes toward asylum, are distasteful to humanitarian organizations. There are good reasons to fear that the tightening of asylum procedures will not only deter abusers of the system but also discourage those who do have a strong claim to refugee status from seeking protection. The recognition is widespread, however, that resettlement on a scale to meet today's mass displacements is not a realistic option and that prevention is better than cure.

Even more fundamental is the development of new thinking about forced displacement as a violation of a person's right *not* to move. Whereas refugee law as it developed after World War II focused on the responsibilities of countries of asylum, today's multilateral emphasis in increasingly directed toward the responsibilities of countries of origin. This is reflected, for example, in the 1990 Paris Declaration of the Conference on Security and Cooperation in Europe (CSCE) which, among other things, recognized that member states should not follow policies that result in a disorderly outflow of their citizens to seek security, shelter, or livelihood in other countries.[12] In 1992 the CSCE appointed a high commissioner for national minorities, with the authority to monitor conditions in member states that in an earlier period would have been regarded as strictly domestic affairs.

Other major hallmarks of evolving policies to deal with displacement include a more assertive attitude toward access for humanitarian organizations to people in need and greater international attention to human rights and the problems of internally displaced people—subjects previously shielded from international scrutiny by the walls of sovereignty. For example, Security Council Resolution 688 of April 5, 1991, insisted "that Iraq allow immediate access by international humanitarian organization to all those in need of assistance in all parts of Iraq and . . . make available all necessary facilities for their operations." Other UN bodies before and since have asserted or aggressively negotiated access for relief supplies and workers, including in conflict situations. There is now a range of experience resulting from the new insistence on humanitarian access. It includes the following:

- *Intervention with the reluctant consent of the parties* (Operation Lifeline Sudan, 1989). Under great pressure from the international community, both the government of Sudan and the Sudan People's Liberation Movement/Army consented to relief being delivered to territories controlled by their opponents.
- *Intervention in the absence of central authority* (Somalia, 1992–1993). After the complete breakdown of law and order following the collapse of the Siad Barre regime in 1991 and the failure of any contending faction to establish dominance, a UN-sanctioned intervention by the United States permitted the resumption of humanitarian assistance throughout the country. A multilateral force later replaced the Americans, though with continued U.S. participation.
- *Intervention without consent but without armed resistance* (northern Iraq, 1991). When coalition forces created a safe haven for the Kurds in northern Iraq, the defeated Iraqi military forces did not attack, although Baghdad protested the violation of its sovereignty in the strongest terms.
- *Intervention met with armed opposition* (Bosnia and Herzegovina, 1992–1993). Relief convoys in the former Yugoslavia are increasingly being targeted by virtually all the parties to the conflict—by Serbs and Croats who see any attempt to assist Bosnian Muslims as an obstacle to ethnic cleansing, and by Muslim forces that see the presence of humanitarian workers on the ground as an obstacle to military intervention to halt or roll back Serb and Croat territorial gains.

No unified code of humanitarian access or intervention has emerged from these disparate experiences. Despite the extreme frustrations of Bosnia and Herzegovina, however, the idea of a "right to assistance" is gaining broader acceptance. In fact, the obligations of states to permit the delivery of relief are central tenets of international humanitarian law, also known as the laws of war. The 1949 Geneva Conventions relating to the Protection of Civilian Persons in Time of War obliges all parties to an international conflict to allow free passage for humanitarian assistance such as food. This provision is reinforced by the two 1977 protocols to the conventions. The second protocol, which deals with the protection of civilians in internal conflicts, also prohibits the starvation of civilians as a method of combat and requires the protection of medical personnel and transport. A tougher insistence on observance of humanitarian law, and surer methods for holding violators accountable for their actions (including war crimes trials where appropriate), would likely reduce the numbers of civilians forced to flee from the secondary effects of armed conflicts.

Multilateral cooperation in response to mass displacements used to be directed almost solely to humanitarian assistance and the provision of asylum. Now, with the shift toward prevention and repatriation, and with most mass displacements arising in a context of armed conflict, it has entered the much more complex realm of "comprehensive response."[13] A comprehensive response is needed for dealing with refugee flows when the following conditions apply:

1. an entire region is affected by a common set of problems;
2. there is enough commonality of interests and incentives within a region to make a multilateral approach promising;
3. humanitarian organizations alone are unable, by themselves, to deal with the major obstacles to protection and solutions; and
4. a bridge is needed between regional and international initiatives.

In recent examples of multilateral engagement in refugee-creating conflicts and their solutions, relief and protection are more and more closely tied to peacekeeping and peacemaking operations. The comprehensive response combines traditional measures of protection, such as asylum abroad, with a more assertive approach to the causes of refugee flows. Whereas international assistance used to be available to refugees only after they had crossed an international border, it is now frequently being delivered within the potential refugee's own country, even in the midst of war.

A number of innovative programs are bringing respite to displaced persons in the context of continuing armed conflict. Humanitarian corridors for delivery of relief supplies worked for a time in Sudan and have been used in Bosnia, where they are plagued with problems. Open Relief Centers in Sri Lanka offer protection to civilians in areas of sporadic fighting and have been respected by both sides. A humanitarian summit for the Horn of Africa held in April 1992 produced new commitments from leaders of governments and opposition groups for free passage of relief supplies.

"Preventive zones" established in Somalia along the Kenyan border give starving civilians an alternative to crossing the border in search of food and allow them to remain in or close to their homes. Proposals to set up safety zones in other war-torn places have generated controversy, however, with critics charging that the idea is motivated more by the desire to keep refugees out of neighboring countries than by concern for their safety. In any case, considerable practical problems surround the establishment of safety zones. There is always a danger that they will become ghettoes, or refugee camps writ large. If they are too small to sustain a working economy, they also could make people permanent wards of the international community. Worse, a safety zone may offer very little safety, as the inhabitants of eastern Bosnian enclaves learned in the summer of 1993.

Sometimes all attempts at prevention, negotiation, and in-country assistance fail to protect civilians. Here, the preservation of the institution of asylum, and continued access to it, remains vital.

The complexity of the causes of emergency population displacement argues for a well-thought-out division of labor among multilateral institutions, but one that allows each agency to retain flexibility. There are some grounds for optimism that this division of labor is beginning to emerge. Coordination among UN agencies is improving not so much because a department of humanitarian affairs was established and given a mandate to coordinate but rather because the agencies have benefited from experience and responded to past criticism. Equally important is better communication between UN agencies such as the UNHCR and non-UN entities such as the International Organization for Migration (IOM) and the International Committee of the Red Cross. These institutions have different mandates, strengths, and philosophies, with the differences as much a source of strength as of weakness for the humanitarian system as a whole. Nongovernmental organizations also come into this picture, often acting with the speed, flexibility, and freedom from political constraints that give them an impact disproportional to their resources.

Humanitarian agencies working in an extreme situation such as that which unfolded in Bosnia and Herzegovina throughout 1993 face unbearable contradictions. Part of their mission is to prevent coerced displacement, yet the UNHCR is being forced to evacuate people from their homes in the face of continued "ethnic cleansing" and the establishment of so-called safe areas such as Srebenica that are little more than extended refugee camps. As the high commissioner put it, "If we participate, we are accessories to ethnic cleansing; if we don't we are accessories to murder."[14] The new emphasis on prevention and repatriation can have meaning only if it is backed up by powerful governments acting in concert.

Multilateral cooperation has produced remarkable capacities for meeting the needs of refugees, especially in the realm of physical relief. The system of humanitarian assistance has saved millions of lives, including hundreds of thousands in the Balkans in 1992-1993, and continues to do so. International efforts have been less successful in preventing the conditions leading to displacement, commanding observance of humanitarian law, and resolving or containing conflicts. Humanitarian assistance even at its best cannot replace the need for political solutions. One of the lessons of Bosnia is the limitations of humanitarian assistance in the face of ruthless antagonists who systematically violate international humanitarian law in the absence of multilateral cooperation to enforce negotiated agreements. UNHCR, as the designated UN "lead agency," has been very clear that its mission in the former Yugoslavia was to buy time for the political negotiations to bring an end the conflict—time in which individuals could be protected and helped to survive until some resolution of the conflict could be achieved and they could resume normal lives. In the absence of such a resolution, more people are displaced, killed, raped, and terrorized every day.

Greater reliance on collective action through multilateral organizations is one of the most positive fruits of the end of the cold war. There are nonetheless at least two distinct kinds of dangers that arise from it that specifically bear on the protection of refugees. Both reflect the fact that multilateral organizations are aggregations of states and are not always greater than the sum of their parts. One danger is that the involvement of a multilateral agency becomes an alibi, or even a reason, for inaction. The presence of an international organization providing humanitarian assistance can soothe the consciences of those who are troubled by political inaction; it also deflects public criticism to some extent. A major constraint on the enforcement of agreements in the former Yugoslavia, for example, is the presence of UN peacekeepers and humanitarian staff on the ground, and the fear that more aggressive intervention would put them in danger of retaliation. They are, in effect, hostages.

The second danger is that negotiations in multilateral organizations can, when there is neither strong consensus nor strong leadership, lead to outcomes that reflect the least common denominator of values or commitments. That is the concern surrounding some of the western European consultations on asylum issues, where measures of harmonization seem to be more restrictive than the prevailing norms. For example, the Dublin Convention and the Schengen

Accord say that asylum applications should be examined by no more than one participating state in order to discourage "asylum shopping," whereas Dutch law requires the government to respond to all asylum claims filed in the Netherlands whether or not they have been heard and rejected elsewhere. European Community harmonization initiatives are much more likely to tighten than to liberalize existing laws and practices.

New approaches are urgently needed to cope with the size and complexity of population movements today. The relatively small proportion of the migratory flows that is made up of refugees has a claim on the international community, which must provide assistance, protection, and above all seek solutions to the causes of their plight. The policymakers and the citizens of western European states are engaged in an intense debate on the role that asylum in Europe should play in meeting this obligation. The debate is entangled in broader questions about the role of immigration in European societies, the security of borders, and humanitarian obligations.

Clearly, asylum in western Europe cannot be a solution for more than a tiny fraction of people affected by violence and conflict in a dangerous world. But it is a lifeline for some, and the institution of asylum is a proud European tradition. Rather than see it buckle under the current strains, European states should redouble their efforts to make it work within a larger response to refugee issues—a response that focuses on preventing and resolving the conflicts and abuses that produce refugees. Such an approach will not only help to solve the asylum crisis; it would contribute directly to European security as well.

Notes

1.   These and other figures in the text, unless otherwise noted, are from UNHCR, *The State of the World's Refugees* (New York: Penguin, 1993).

2.   The 1951 Convention defines a refugee as one who, "owing to a well-founded fear of persecution for reasons of race, religion, nationality, membership of a particular social group or political opinion, is outside the country of his nationality and is unable or, owing to such fear, unwilling to avail himself of the protection of that country."

3.   Emigrants from China, however, have received a much more variable reception.

4.   Temporary asylum is also used to permit people who have been denied refugee status, but would face danger if returned to their country of origin, to remain on a temporary basis.

5. Figures on the former Soviet republics are from the U.S. Committee for Refugees, *World Refugee Survey, 1992* (Washington, D.C.: USCR, 1992).

6. The nine are Belgium, France, Germany, Greece, Italy, Luxembourg, the Netherlands, Portugal, and Spain. (See *Financial Times*, July 1, 1993.)

7. Ian Davidson, "Europe Tries to Shut the Floodgates," *Financial Times*, June 3, 1993.

8. James C. Hathaway, "The Emerging Politics of Non-entree," *Refugees*, no. 91 (December 1992): 40–41.

9. USCR, *World Refugee Survey, 1993.*

10. United Nations Convention Relating to the Status of Refugees, Article 31.1.

11. Sadako Ogata, "Refugees: A Comprehensive European Strategy" (statement at the Peace Palace, The Hague, Netherlands, November 24, 1992).

12. Guy S. Goodwin-Gill, "Towards a Comprehensive Regional Policy Approach: The Case for Closer Inter-Agency Cooperation" (paper presented for the UNHCR and the IOM at the Human Dimension Seminar of Migration, Including Refugees and Displaced Persons, Conference on Security and Cooperation in Europe, Warsaw, April 1993).

13. See, for example, UNHCR, "A Comprehensive Response to the Humanitarian Crisis in the former Yugoslavia" (paper presented to the International Meeting on Humanitarian Aid for Victims of the Conflict in the former Yugoslavia, Geneva, July 29, 1992).

14. Sadako Ogata, conversation with author, Washington, D.C., May 26, 1993.

5

Migration and Economic Intervention

Sidney Weintraub and Georges A. Fauriol

Concern over the inflow of "unwanted" immigrants has become intense in western Europe and is increasing in the United States and even Japan. The word *unwanted* refers to persons who enter a foreign country without an immigration visa or, if a refugee seeking asylum, cannot demonstrate a well-founded fear of persecution.[1]

The demand for action to limit the entry of persons who enter without documents (EWI in official U.S. immigration parlance), or who seek formal status as refugees, has been most pronounced during the past few years in western Europe, where events have conspired to augment the flow of migrants. In addition, despite the presence and entry of many foreigners, western European states do not consider themselves to be "immigration countries"—that is, nations that welcome a large flow of "wanted" immigrants for permanent residence. Much the same is true in Japan, although the inflow of unwanted foreigners is still relatively small there.[2]

The United States, however, is an immigrant country, but the apparent increase in undocumented immigration during the past several years, coupled with persistently high domestic unemployment, has given this issue political salience once again.[3] The anti-immigration issue—especially as it relates to undocumented immigrants—is never far below the surface in the United States, although it is less intense here than in western Europe.[4] This difference can be explained less by absolute numbers than by the combination in Europe of the rate of entries in some countries and the general philosophy of welcome or rejection of permanent immigrants. Nevertheless, the United States can be most unwelcoming toward certain immigrants. The Haitian boat people are the prime example.

Unwanted immigrants can be kept out in a number of ways, at least in principle. They can be turned back at or near borders, or on the high seas in the case of Haitians, but this is costly and difficult. The U.S. border with Mexico is too lengthy to be easily patrolled. Would-be immigrants can be screened after entry, which is the main practice in Germany for refugees, but this raises complex issues of determining motivation and therefore the right of permanent asylum. National political considerations inevitably enter into this process; the United States, for example, is more welcoming to Cuban refugees than to Haitian. In the case of Haitians, the United States has opted for refugee screening in Haiti, which raises self-evident issues of due process when the motive is to escape from a country where one fears persecution. Employers who knowingly hire undocumented aliens can be fined, a technique adopted with indifferent success in both Europe and the United States.

Finally, the effort to turn off migration pressures can be focused on the sending areas through various forms of economic intervention or, perhaps phrased better, economic *cooperation*. This last technique is the theme of this paper. There is some comparison in what follows between the European and U.S. efforts at economic intervention in sending countries, but the stress is on U.S. efforts. The next section sets the dimensions of the problem by providing data on immigration into the United States. A discussion of the central subject of this paper follows—namely, the techniques of economic cooperation and what results might be expected from them. Two specific cases of special interest for the United States—Haiti and Cuba—are presented separately.

Data on Immigration into the United States

The United States in recent years has admitted between 600,000 and 700,000 immigrants a year for permanent residence. At the upper end, this is less than 0.3 percent of the U.S. population. Over a decade, however, this comes to between 2 and 3 percent of the U.S. population (see tables 5.1 and 5.2). The immigrant admissions of recent years have been temporarily inflated by the legalization of millions of persons pursuant to the Immigration Reform and Control Act (IRCA) of 1986 (see table 5.1).

Of the nonlegalization admissions, the bulk fall under various provisions of U.S. legislation dealing with family unification. Most permanent immigration visas are now issued to persons from Latin America and the Caribbean and secondarily from Asia. This is evident from table 5.3. The 1990 and 1991 proportions for Latin America and the Caribbean, however, are inflated because more than 90 percent of the legalization applications came from this region, primarily Mexico. By the same token, the proportion of legal permanent immigrants admitted from Asia during those years is distorted.

Table 5.1
Immigrants Admitted to the United States,
Fiscal Years 1990 and 1991
(in thousands of persons)

	1990	1991[a]
Total	1,536	1,827
of which:		
legalization[b]	880	1,123
nonlegalization	656	704

Source: U.S. Immigration and Naturalization Service (INS), *Statistical Yearbook of the Immigration and Naturalization Service, 1991* (Washington, D.C.: U.S. Government Printing Office, 1992), 22.
[a] U.S. fiscal year 1991 runs from October 1, 1990, to September 30, 1991.
[b] This term refers to persons granted legal permanent resident status under the Immigration Reform and Control Act of 1986. Of these in 1991, 214,003 were legalized because of residence in the United States since 1982, and 909,159 were legalized under the Special Agricultural Worker provisions of the act.

Table 5.2
Flow of Legal Immigrants into the United States,
by Decades, 1901–1990
(in millions of persons)

Period	Immigrants Admitted
1901–1910	8.8
1911–1920	5.7
1921–1930	4.1
1931–1940	0.5
1941–1950	1.0
1951–1960	2.5
1961–1970	3.3
1971–1980	4.5
1981–1990	7.3

Source: Elizabeth S. Ralph, *Immigration Policies: Legacy from the 1980s and Issues for the 1990s* (Santa Monica, Calif.: RAND, 1992), 21, based on data from the *Statistical Abstract of the United States, 1991.*

Table 5.3
Region of Last Residence of Legal Immigrants to the United States, Fiscal Years 1901 to 1991
(percent)

Decade	Europe	Asia	Western Hemisphere[a]	Other[b]
1901–1910	92	4	4	–
1911–1920	75	4	20	1
1921–1930	60	3	37	–
1931–1940	66	3	30	1
1941–1950	60	4	34	2
1951–1960	53	6	40	1
1961–1970	34	13	52	2
1971–1980	18	35	44	3
1981–1990	10	37	49	3
Year				
1990	8	21	68	3
1991	8	19	71	2

Source: INS, *Statistical Yearbook, 1991,* table 2.
Note: Numbers may not add to total due to rounding.
[a] Immigrants from Canada in this category gradually declined in relative importance in comparison with those from Latin America and the Caribbean.
[b] Includes mainly Africa and Oceania, of which the African proportion increased over time.

The decline in the proportion of immigrants coming from Europe has been quite dramatic over the course of this century. More than half of U.S. immigrant visas were issued to Europeans as recently as 50 years ago, compared with about 10 percent today. Most asylum approvals are still given to persons from eastern Europe and the former Soviet Union, but the absolute numbers are relatively small compared with permanent residence visas granted and the inflow of undocumented aliens (see table 5.4 for U.S. refugee approvals).

Table 5.4
U.S. Refugee Approvals by Geographic Area,
Fiscal Years 1984–1991
(in thousands of persons)

Year	Total	Africa	East Asia	Eastern Europe and USSR	Latin America and Caribbean	Near East
1984	78	3	59	11	–	5
1985	59	2	40	10	2	6
1986	52	1	35	10	–	6
1987	62	2	37	12	–	10
1988	80	1	41	27	2	8
1989	96	2	35	49	3	7
1990	100	3	31	59	2	5
1991	108	4	34	63	2	5

Source: INS, *Statistical Yearbook, 1991,* table 26.

This shift toward Latin America in issuing immigrant visas is one factor contributing to the steady change in the ethnic mix of the United States. Another is the inflow of undocumented immigrants (see table 5.5). More than 85 percent of aliens (more than 1 million individuals) apprehended in U.S. fiscal year 1991 after unlawful entry were from Latin American countries; almost 95 percent of the apprehensions were from Mexico alone. According to the 1990 census, the growth of the Latino population of the United States was five times greater than for the U.S.population as a whole—53 percent for the Latino population between 1980 and 1990 compared with 10 percent for the total population. For the first time in U.S. history, Hispanics outnumber African Americans and constitute the largest minority in the United States (*CBS News,* September 27, 1993). Legalizations under IRCA will intensify this Latinization of the United States in the years ahead as these persons, now legal permanent residents, petition for immigrant visas for their families.

Table 5.5
Aliens Apprehended in the United States,
Fiscal Years 1931–1991
(in thousands of persons)

Decade	Apprehended	Year	Apprehended
1931–1940	147	1986	1,767
1941–1950	1,377	1987	1,190
1951–1960	3,599	1988	1,008
1961–1970	1,608	1989	954
1971–1980	8,321	1990	1,170
1981–1990	11,888	1991	1,198

Source: INS, *Statistical Yearbook, 1991*, table 55.

IRCA was enacted in 1986. Two of its main features were the imposition of penalties against employers who knowingly hire illegal aliens and the legalization of persons resident in the United States since 1982 or who met certain conditions as agricultural workers. Apprehensions of undocumented aliens fell off sharply beginning in 1987 but then began to increase again in 1990. The initial decline in apprehensions is easily understandable because the legalization features of the act, particularly the Special Agricultural Workers (SAWs) program, offered a relatively easy and preferable alternative for entry into the United States—preferable because it provided legal residence. As the legalizations have run their course, earlier patterns of entry into the United States seem to be recurring. IRCA did not call for a verifiable identity card, and documents provided to employers to show a legal right to be in the United States were easily forged. In addition, enforcement of the employer penalty provisions was not stringent and most penalties were modest.

Some comparative data may help to indicate the different contexts of western Europe and the United States. The U.S. population is roughly 250 million and that of the receiving countries in western Europe (the countries of the European Community [EC] and the European Free Trade Association [EFTA] combined) is about 365 million. The number of asylum claims in western Europe was around 900,000 in 1992, about half of them in Germany alone.[5] The increase in asylum seekers in Germany has been dramatic: under 100,000 a year during most of the 1980s, 103,000 in 1988, and

430,000 in 1992. Although the German rejection rate has been high, between 90 and 95 percent, the evaluation process can be time-consuming, lasting one or more years. It is this increase, and fear of further increases owing to unsettled conditions in eastern Europe and the former Soviet Union, that led to the clamor to change the German constitution to permit more rapid repatriation of most asylum seekers.

By contrast, the number of asylum seekers in France, the other major destination in the EC for this category of immigrants, has been declining. Asylum seekers in France numbered 61,372 in 1989, 47,380 in 1991, and fell again in 1992. In 1991, France admitted about 125,000 persons for legal immigration, about 58,000 under family reunification provisions, fewer than 50,000 asylum seekers, and about 25,000 as legalized workers (including some asylum seekers formerly rejected). Although the countries of western Europe do not consider themselves to be immigration countries, immigration is taking place through family reunification, persons seeking asylum, worker legalization, and unlawful entry. The absolute numbers actually granted permanent residence are lower than in the United States as a proportion of total population, but they are not negligible.[6]

Economic Cooperation with Sending Countries

The steady relative decline of legal immigration into the United States from Europe, coupled with the growing number of asylum seekers in western Europe, shows that economic development can convert countries from net senders of migrants to receivers of immigrants (see table 5.3). This is the rationale for programs of economic intervention or cooperation between migrant-sending and migrant-receiving countries. The policy instruments of economic cooperation are trade, investment, and foreign aid.[7] European countries are using a combination of all these instruments, sometimes quite deliberately with immigration-stanching measures in mind. The stress, however, has been on aid techniques.[8] The U.S. emphasis of recent years, by contrast, has been on trade and investment measures.

A word of caution is needed on U.S. motives. When the United States initiated the Caribbean Basin Initiative (CBI) in the 1980s, President Ronald Reagan made a passing reference to its potential immigration-dampening effect, but this was not its central purpose. Similarly, although official U.S. justification for a free trade agreement with Mexico alluded to the potential of free trade in discouraging emigration pressure in Mexico by raising incomes there, this objective has not been paramount. U.S. foreign economic policy is driven by economic and political motives, and migration issues enter into the policy-making process only tangentially, perhaps when a policy based on other motives needs justification for public relations purposes.[9]

Yet the migration consequences of the proposed North American Free Trade Agreement (NAFTA) scream out for analysis. This agreement focuses on economic integration with the country that sends more migrants, legal and otherwise, to the United States than any other country. The centerpiece of the agreement is on trade and investment relations with Mexico. It has no migration provisions other than those dealing with temporary entry for businesspersons. NAFTA has no explicit aid component. It is therefore unlike trade agreements among EC countries, which provide for resource transfers from richer to poorer countries and from wealthier to more laggard regions.

Beyond that, despite EC provisions allowing migration among member countries, there is in fact much more migration from Mexico to the United States than takes place within the EC. The situation in Europe would be more comparable to that proposed between Mexico and the United States if the EC were to enter into comprehensive economic integration agreements with Turkey and countries in eastern Europe and the former Soviet Union, the source of the EC's unwanted migrants.

The Migration Consequences of NAFTA

Several major analyses conclude that although economic development is the crucial variable in reducing Mexico's emigration pressure, it may actually accelerate emigration in the short term. The reasoning is that social and economic development raises horizons and gives individuals and families the means to migrate across borders before the countervailing income effects provide sufficient incentive to stay home.[10] Douglas Massey comes to this conclusion after examining the path of European emigration.[11]

Several analysts push this point further in the case of NAFTA. Philip Martin gives two reasons to expect short-term immigration into the United States from Mexico to increase: the displacement of millions of persons from rural Mexico during the next 10 to 15 years and the probability that persons who move to the border to work in *maquiladora* (export-processing) plants use this as a stepping-stone for emigrating to the United States.[12] Hinojosa and Robinson, using general equilibrium modeling, conclude that the changes in Mexican agricultural policy in the wake of NAFTA will lead some 800,000 additional migrants to enter the United States.[13]

Recent developments provide some support for these contentions of short-term migration increases. The increase in alien apprehensions since 1990 (see table 5.5) has coincided with an upturn in the Mexican economy, which began to gather steam only in 1990.[14] This, however, is not sturdy evidence of the likelihood of short-term migration increases. Apprehensions are being used here as a proxy for the direction in which undocumented immigration is moving—that is, whether it is increasing or decreasing. Although accurate, it is only a rough measure. Simultaneous measurement of economic performance and emigration flows—using the year 1991 for each—is too short term to have great significance. And, as noted earlier, the undocumented migration flows of 1990 and 1991 were distorted by the U.S. legalization program.

Other questions can be raised about the hypothesis of inevitable short-term increases as economic conditions improve in the sending country. Massey's evidence is quite powerful in that social and economic development in Europe did stimulate emigration, but data from the nineteenth century can be only suggestive and not conclusive for the current period, when the phenomenon of unwanted immigration is much more intense. It is also quite hard to know when the short-term emigration stimulus of economic growth is transformed into the long-term decision to stay home.

The conclusions of Martin and Hinojosa-Robinson are driven by expected rural to urban movement in Mexico that will then spill over into migration into the United States. This, by itself, is a reasonable conclusion; evidence over decades shows that immigration into the United States originates mainly in rural Mexico. It is more questionable, however, to attribute the accelerated exodus from rural areas to NAFTA, as both studies do. The change in land tenure in Mexico, plus the curtailment of producer subsidies, which is driving the expected shift from the land, is not attributable solely to NAFTA. Indeed, the change in the *ejido* system of land tenure is unrelated to any NAFTA commitment made by Mexico.

The change in subsidy policy affects mainly corn production.[15] Some 2-3 million Mexicans grow corn on small plots or work in corn-growing areas. Most of these farms are on nonirrigated land. Inhabitants of Mexico's rain-fed, rural areas are the nation's poorest citizens. They have inadequate diets and poor or inadequate schooling. They are leaving the land in any event out of economic necessity. The producer subsidies that are gradually being removed benefit mainly wealthy growers who use irrigated land in northern Mexico. The consumer subsidies that compensate for the producer subsidies are designed to keep corn (and tortilla) prices low in the cities and do not benefit most Mexicans who live and work in the country's rain-fed, rural areas.

The plan to liberalize corn imports in NAFTA over a 15-year transition period coincides with a policy that the Mexican authorities wish to institute in any event. It is thus hard to attribute rural to urban migration outcomes in Mexico, and then migration out of the country, to NAFTA. Mexican agricultural policy may accelerate this international migration, but that will depend on economic outturn within Mexico itself. Beyond this uncertainty, there is no convincing indication of how Hinojosa and Robinson determined that NAFTA would lead to 800,000 additional migrants to the United States.

Martin refers to the stepping-stone migration from the interior of Mexico to *maquiladora* plants at the border and then into the United States as one potential consequence of NAFTA. As his study admits, this is an intuitive conclusion—his reasoning is that if Mexicans move to the border, and then learn of the higher income they can earn by crossing it, they will do so. The evidence, as he also admits, does not support this stepping-stone conclusion.[16]

Even more to the point, because Martin's intuition may be correct, the salience of *maquiladoras* will diminish under NAFTA. Production in these plants now enjoy entry into the United States by paying the import duty only on the valued added outside the United States. Under NAFTA, almost all Mexican production will enjoy duty-free entry into the United States after a transition period. NAFTA, if anything, will reduce whatever stepping-stone effect the *maquiladoras* have. If a plant is at the border, it might be a stepping-stone. If workers have come to cities from rural areas in Mexico, the cities, wherever located, can be stepping-stones. The *maquiladoras*, in other words, become largely irrelevant in a study on the migration outcomes of NAFTA.

The Wage Differential and NAFTA

If international migration is the consequence largely of wage differentials, as most research shows, the question of how NAFTA might affect wages in the two countries gets to the heart of the matter.[17] According to the U.S. Bureau of Labor Statistics (BLS), hourly compensation costs for production workers in manufacturing in Mexico was 14 percent of the costs in the United States, roughly a seven to

Table 5.6
Annual Percentage Changes in Compensation Costs, 1989–1991

	1989	1990	1991
United States	2.9	4.0	3.8
Mexico	20.5	13.2	20.6

Source: U.S. Bureau of Labor Statistics, "International Comparisons of Hourly Compensation Costs for Production Workers in Manufacturing, 1991," Report 825, June 1992, p. 7.

one ratio.[18] In absolute terms, the amounts were $15.45 in the United States and $2.17 in Mexico. These are what the BLS calls total compensation costs and include direct pay and insurance and benefit plans. Despite their seeming precision, these figures are inexact because of exchange-rate anomalies in the commercial market. In addition, they do not capture differences in the cost of living. The figure $2.17 translates into about $87 for a 40-hour week, and this will buy more in purchasing power in Mexico that would the same income in most parts of the United States.

Compensation in Mexico, after adjusting for inflation, declined by about 40 percent from 1982 until about 1988, which were the worst years of economic depression. Real wages started to rise again in 1989. Table 5.6 compares these increases with U.S. wage changes.

What evidence shows is that Mexican wages are responsive to economic conditions in the country. The drop in real wages during the difficult economic years was exaggerated by government policy that deliberately sought to limit the increase in open unemployment. The institutional structure of organized labor in Mexico, where the key union confederation is largely an arm of the official party, the Institutional Revolutionary Party (PRI), facilitated this strategy. The sharp increases from 1989 to 1991 were a reflection not only of increased economic activity, but also of recuperating past declines and lower inflation.

Wage behavior in Mexico is also influenced by the large cohorts entering the labor force. The fertility rate in Mexico has declined significantly since the 1970s and it is now calculated that annual population increases are about 2 percent a year and declining, compared with about 3 percent before the 1970s.[19] Because those born earlier when fertility rates were higher are now coming of age, however, about 1 million persons enter the labor force each year.

This is over and above open unemployment in urban areas, which is officially measured at around 3 percent of the economically active population (which is about 30 million), plus high rates of underemployment in rural areas, plus increased entry of women into the labor force, plus the informal economy, which is estimated at 25 percent of the total employed population.[20] In good years, the United States creates about 2 million jobs a year with a population of 250 million. Mexico must create more than half this number of jobs each year for a population numbering 85 million. It is hardly surprising that much of the labor force crosses over the border into the United States.

The large labor supply undoubtedly acts as a drag on wage increases, particularly for unskilled workers. Complaints are heard regularly in Mexico that productivity increases do not translate into wage increases, at least not very quickly, and this has the ring of truth because of the excess labor supply. And yet it is hard to see how emigration pressures can be dampened unless substantial job creation and steady increases in real wages occur. Based on historical data, the absorption of 1 million new job seekers each year requires overall growth of gross domestic product (GDP) of about 5 to 6 percent. This translates into 3 percent job growth in an economically active population of about 30 million, or about half the rate of growth of GDP.

This need for GDP growth to absorb labor and raise real wages must be related to the economic model adopted by Mexico during the 1980s. Mexico shifted its economic policy from looking inward by protecting domestic industry to looking outward. Put somewhat more technically, the bias against exports was transformed into one in favor of exports. The growth in GDP since about 1989 has taken place under the new model, but the experiment has yet to run its course. GDP growth was deliberately slowed to about 2.6 percent in 1992 to restrain inflation and to reduce the growing deficit in the current account of the balance of payments, and this resulted in only a modest growth in GDP per capita.

The emphasis on exports must inevitably focus on the U.S. market. In a normal year about 70 percent of Mexico's exports are sent to the United States. For manufactured goods the percentage is upwards of 80 percent. This is the proper measure because Mexico's oil exports, which are still large, have a worldwide market. Manufactured exports, by contrast, are largely intrafirm, often in the form of intermediate products. These exports rely on prior foreign investment and various forms of coproduction between plants in the United States and Mexico.

A straightforward triad can thus be given:

1. There is no way for Mexico to reach its GDP growth targets without open access to the U.S. market for its exports.
2. There is no way for Mexico to absorb its growing labor force without high rates of growth of GDP.
3. There is no way to dampen the pressure for emigration from Mexico without providing good jobs at home.

NAFTA is a logical response to the first imperative of this triad. NAFTA, viewed from this perspective, is an insurance policy against potential U.S. protectionism. It is designed to attract foreign investment for coproduction on the assurance of a large, combined North American market of 360 million people with close to $7 trillion of GDP. NAFTA itself is not the source of future growth of GDP, although its existence can accelerate growth, but rather a supplement to internal economic policy.

One additional question must be asked: if the Mexican economy grows at a rate fast enough to absorb new entrants in the labor market, will wages, salaries, and income rise sufficiently to make these jobs attractive, to keep people at home? The answer is not self-evident. If the Mexican economy grows by 5 to 6 percent a year, skill shortages will appear. This is already happening in major industrial areas around Monterrey. As the backlog in the labor supply is diminished, real wages will certainly rise, as they have been doing in recent years. The Mexican advantage today in attracting foreign investment is its low wages. This is hardly a recipe for the indefinite future. As wages rise, the gap between U.S. and Mexican wages should diminish. As this occurs, Mexico will have to shed much of its low-wage attraction.

If the development strategy, of which NAFTA is a part, succeeds, the Mexican development path should resemble that of South Korea, through an upgrading of production toward more sophisticated products. This is already taking place. The co-production arrangements in the automotive industry require more training and greater skills—and provide higher wages—than in older, traditional consumer industries. The *maquiladoras* used to specialize in clothing production. Transportation and electronic equipment now far outstrip clothing production. The labor force of the *maquiladoras* used to be upwards of 90 percent women; the male-female ratio is now almost identical. A country cannot sustain long-term development without upgrading the skills, and with that the wages, of its population.

The third part of the triad relates to the effect of jobs and rising wages on emigration. How long will it take for this combination to have its effect? The answer is not clear. If Massey and the Commission for the Study of International Migration and Cooperative Economic Development (CSIMCED) are correct, there will either be an upsurge or no diminution in Mexican emigration over some undefined short term. Yet recently we have seen countries move from emigration to immigration status in a few decades. Italy is an example of this. Spain may no longer be an emigration country.

There is no standard for what income or wage differential induces international migration.[21] Population movements are sometimes large with small income differentials and modest with fairly large ones. Migration from Europe to the United States dropped sharply long before income differentials were eliminated. Perhaps the most important of the other determining factors is the expectation of potential migrants of opportunities at home for themselves and their children. Will they be able to find employment at a decent wage in their own country? If they are more skilled, what career opportunities exist at home? If they are parents, what educational opportunities are their children afforded? Each person answers these questions not merely on the basis of his or her income differential for potential employment in the United States, but also on some judgment of the pattern of future economic and social development at home. If Mexican GDP rises by 5 percent a year, year after year, that then could become the norm for expectations. This takes time—at least 5years, perhaps 10 or more. In any event, incentives to remain in Mexico can become quite powerful long before incomes there reach the level in the United States.

This is the promise of economic cooperation, which Mexico requires if its economic strategy is to succeed. Failing this cooperation, there is little prospect that emigration pressure will diminish. With it, it is just possible that Mexico will meet its development objectives and that this, in time, will dampen the urge to cross over into the United States. It is hard to predict how long this will take. Yet there is no viable alternative unless there is a radical transformation of the relationship involving a more fortified frontier and a rigorous U.S. program of employer penalties for hiring illegal workers, made effective by a foolproof national identity system. Even such drastic measures by no means ensure success.

The Caribbean Basin Initiative

The countries of the Caribbean Basin—those in the Caribbean proper and in Central America—are important sending areas to the United States, both for legal and unauthorized immigration. Five of these countries—Haiti, El Salvador, the Dominican Republic, Guatemala, and Jamaica, whose combined population is only 31 million—were among the top 15 from which legal immigrants were admitted in U.S. fiscal year 1991. Caribbean Basin nationals also figure prominently in expulsions for being illegally in the United States, although their numbers are dwarfed by Mexicans.[22]

Anthony Maingot has pointed out that there is a true subculture of migration in the Caribbean.[23] The countries are quite small and provide limited career opportunities. Habits of migration have thus become ingrained. Emigration from Central America to the United States was less ingrained until the civil turmoil in the region, particularly in the 1980s, stimulated flight. Extensive networks now exist between Central America and the United States, and now that the spigot of emigration is open, it will be difficult to close.

The CBI was a form of U.S. economic intervention designed to stimulate job creation through one-way trade preferences to beneficiary countries. The initiative had some effect in stimulating investment and exports from the region to the United States, but its major shortcoming was that it excluded many of the region's most competitive exports from preferential treatment.[24]

NAFTA relies on trade and investment cooperation for stimulating economic development in Mexico. The CBI does the same, although in a more limited way. In addition to these instruments, however, the United States does supply aid to Caribbean and Central American countries,[25] although the effectiveness of these economic instruments has been limited by the political turmoil in the region—in Haiti and throughout most of Central America.

The Central American and Caribbean countries may also be adversely affected by NAFTA. Close to 50 percent of the exports of these countries are sent to the United States. The most dynamic of these exports have been clothing and other products produced in export-processing zones. These countries fear that NAFTA will divert investment to Mexico because U.S. import restrictions on apparel products will gradually disappear under NAFTA. Mexico may also have preferential treatment over Caribbean and Central American countries after a transition period for sugar shipped to the United States. The Caribbean and Central American countries are therefore seeking some adjustment in the treatment they receive under the CBI to put them on a par with Mexico. It is possible, however, that as Mexican wages increase, foreign investment in labor-intensive production, such as apparel, will shift to Central American and Caribbean countries.

Two countries in the Caribbean present special problems, actual or potential, of migration to the United States. Both Haiti and Cuba have come to represent the political and moral dilemmas the United States faces in the Caribbean. Cuban migration trends are part of the broader U.S.-Cuban strategic relationship shaped since 1959 by the Castro government. For its part, Haitian migration is part and parcel of that country's political convulsions since the early 1980s. Much less so than Mexican migration, Haitian and Cuban flows have become high drama, involving refugee crises whose dynamics have become highly emotional.

During the 1980 Mariel boatlift, 125,000 Cubans arrived in Florida in just four months, when Fidel Castro allowed (some say forced) political dissidents, felons, mental patients, and generally unhappy Cubans to leave Cuba. This led to the worst immigration crisis the United States had faced since the Indochina boatlift of the mid- and late 1970s. This overwhelmed the state of Florida's capability to process the newly arrived immigrants and also helped to cripple the reelection bid of President Jimmy Carter.

In the fall of 1980, following worsening economic circumstances in Haiti, a flow of "boat people" to the Bahamas and the shores of Florida also caught the world's attention. Late that year, up to 1,500 Haitians a month were arriving in Florida. After a brief physical exam and processing, most were released, their legal status to be determined later.

Ten years and several waves of smaller refugee flows later, Cuba and Haiti still challenge the essence of U.S. immigration policy. The political context that triggers these movements of population is beyond the immediate control of U.S. policy, yet the United States is itself the immediate target of opportunity for these migration flows. The somewhat regulated and bureaucratized U.S. system has been stretched beyond its limits in these circumstances. Highlighting the dilemma is that, unlike the European experience, the United States still considers itself a nation of immigrants.

This has taken on particular political salience given that one of the initial items to be faced by the new White House was Haiti. Indeed, policies that critics of the Bush administration hoped Bill Clinton would modify have included Haiti and Cuba. But in both cases, a considerable degree of continuity is to be found.

So far the practice of returning boat people to Haiti without allowing them to apply for political asylum has been sustained. This has been a bit awkward in that it has put President Clinton in the position of defending a policy that he opposed as a candidate; the future president probably reacted in the campaign on the basis of principle without a sufficient understanding of the practicality. But the Haitian problem, because it defies any simple solution, is an issue the administration may have to revisit.

A similar, but for the moment less critical, duality affects policy toward Cuba. Primarily for what appeared to be electoral objectives, Candidate Clinton outflanked President George Bush in taking a harder line toward Cuba—in effect, endorsing the position of the more conservative elements of the Cuban-American community in Miami, and equally significantly, the position of Rep. Robert G. Torricelli (D-N.J.), the House's ranking voice on Latin American policy (and author of a 1992 bill that tightens the screws on the Castro regime).

The outlook for Haiti is grim and for Cuba, uncertain.[26] The catastrophic Haitian economy has a backdrop of chronic political crises and a serious environmental challenge. Combined, this ensures continuing migration flows toward the United States (see table 5.7). If the last decade is any indication, the ability of U.S. policy to alleviate this process appears realistically limited. What is certain is that Washington's involvement will first and foremost require a political component. Economic policy intervention is only a necessary second step to the degree that it requires at least a semblance of consensus among Haiti's competing political factions. Such consensus does not yet exist. Europe plays a part here because some in Washington argue quietly that major actors such as France have not been as helpful as, perhaps, they could have been on such issues as the enforcement of the economic embargo (which the EC has not endorsed, let alone enforced).

Cuba presents a different challenge. Rumblings, some from Fidel Castro himself, suggest a major crisis for the regime sooner rather than later. But exactly how and when has become the basis of a small cottage industry of Cuba watchers. A by-product of the cold war, Cuban migrants continue to enter the United States under a special status that in effect makes them almost automatically refugees from a Communist regime. There is in this relic of the past a point of tension relevant to the domestic social dynamics of the United States: Cuban refugees still get a hero's welcome, but those from Haiti are most often not even granted "refugee" status, leading to unpleasant charges of racial discrimination and uneven enforcement of U.S. immigration laws. This line of thinking has been boosted by the numerous images of Haitian boat people being forcibly repatriated.

Table 5.7
Immigrants and Refugees Admitted to the United States

A. Immigrants Admitted by Country or Region of Birth

Country/Region	1982	1984	1986	1988	1990	1991
Mexico	56,106	57,557	66,533	95,039	679,068	946,167
Caribbean	67,379	74,265	101,632	112,357	115,351	140,139
Cuba	8,209	10,599	33,114	17,558	10,645	10,349
Haiti	8,779	9,839	12,666	34,806	20,324	47,527
Central America	23,626	24,088	28,380	30,715	146,202	111,093
El Salvador	7,107	8,787	10,929	12,045	80,173	47,351

B. Refugees Admitted by Country of Citizenship

Country/Region	1983	1984	1986	1988	1990	1991
Mexico	7	11	4	5	19	10
Caribbean	943	94	224	3,020	3,999	3,928
Cuba	940	86	213	3,006	3,980	3,910
Haiti	2	4	8	7	4	4
Central America	71	183	178	1,283	1,598	1,128
El Salvador	54	61	26	60	136	110
Haitians rescued by Coast Guard	-	2,951	3,176	4,699	1,131	31,401
Cuban Arrivals— interceptions by any source	19	27	44	467	2,608	-

Source: INS, *Statistical Yearbook*, various editions.

A longer-range feature of the Cuban question relates to the impact that a political reintegration of the island into the region would have on the Caribbean economy. The assumption is usually made that a politically revitalized Cuba would have a positive effect first and foremost on Cuba itself, and in turn would dramatically pump life into the U.S.-Cuban economic relationship. Access to the U.S. market would in fact lead to a drastic modification of U.S.-Caribbean trade patterns, drawn up for the past three decades to bypass Cuba. It is likely that a new Cuban government would aspire to accede to arrangements such as NAFTA or other regional agreement that would link up with Cuba's manufacturing and assembly potential and capitalize on the island's geographical location. How this would effect on the rest of the region is unclear, but there are already quiet expressions of concern among CARICOM (Caribbean Community and Common Market) countries. They correctly fear the competitive pull of a modernizing and much larger Cuban economy for foreign investment, foreign assistance, tourist dollars, and so forth. With average unemployment rates in the 30 percent range throughout much of the region today, the labor market outlook is dim and prospects for migration a certainty well into the next century.

Cuba will most likely benefit uniquely from its extensive and fairly successful exile community, particularly in the United States. Although there is likely to be political tension regarding the role of the Cuban-American community, there is no doubt that it will be a significant economic force. A recent study conducted by the Center for Strategic and International Studies estimates that remittances from Cubans abroad could amount to $800 million a year in the initial years after political change in Cuba.[27] There are currently 1.1 million Cuban-Americans, and it is assumed that some would return to Cuba, although in the first year or two political uncertainties and economic restructuring would trigger an outflow *from* Cuba.

Conclusions

The United States now willingly receives many immigrants from Mexico, but there are also hundreds of thousands of Mexicans who are unwanted immigrants, at least from the national perspective. The options for keeping out the latter range from militant control of the border, to severe penalties against employers who knowingly hire them, to seeking out techniques for economic cooperation that will eventually reduce the pressure for emigration. The first two have been tried with minimal success. The third, in the form of the North American Free Trade Agreement, finally was approved by the U.S. Congress in late 1993 after a drawn-out political battle.

Three imperatives must guide U.S. economic policy toward Mexico. These are that Mexico will not prosper unless the U.S. market remains open; if Mexico does not prosper, it cannot absorb its young and rapidly growing labor force; and if job opportunities are lacking at home, the overflow will surely end up in the United States.

Mexican economic strategy, of which NAFTA is a part, may help resolve the negative aspects of this triad. If economic growth is high enough, say 5 to 6 percent a year, this will absorb labor in jobs that pay much more than Mexican workers now earn. In time, this should reduce unwanted immigration from Mexico. Economic benefits will redound to the United States as the Mexican economy grows—witness the increased U.S. exports of recent years. But beyond this, if the issue is dampening the emigration pressure, the United States has little choice but to foster this development cooperation with Mexico.

The options open to the United States for Central American and Caribbean countries are more problematic. These countries are not now ready for free trade, although an offer was placed on the table from the Bush administration. The preferences these countries now enjoy in the U.S. market under the CBI may be eroded by preferences to Mexico under NAFTA. The two most difficult countries are Cuba, where the migration issue may (or may not) resolve itself once Castro goes because of the potential for economic development; and Haiti, where the prospects for economic growth are dim at best.

The U.S.-Mexico and western Europe–eastern Europe comparison is apt in some respects. As the East develops, its imports will come mainly from western Europe, just as Mexican development has stimulated imports from the United States. The ratio of wages in the receiving countries in western Europe and the sending countries in eastern Europe, including the European part of the former Soviet Union, is 10 to 1.[28] This is higher than the 7 to 1 ratio for manufacturing jobs in the United States and Mexico. If the wage differential is the critical variable in stimulating migration, it is not surprising that so many persons from eastern Europe are seeking refuge in western Europe.

Another similarity in West European and U.S. relations with the major migrant-sending countries is that each will benefit from economic growth in the respective sending countries. Mexico buys most of its imports from the United States. These have skyrocketed in recent years as overall Mexican GDP rose. Western European exports to eastern Europe will similarly benefit disproportionately as the economies in the latter region improve. Finally, rightly or wrongly, the countries of western Europe wish to limit immigration from the East, just as the United States does from Mexico.

But there are also differences. The United States does admit substantial legal immigration from Mexico. Legal immigrants, other than those legalized under IRCA, have averaged about 60,000 a year for at least the past 10 years. If the IRCA legalization immigrants are included, the average annual admissions from Mexico in the three years from 1989 to 1991 were 676,000. This dwarfs the legal admissions into western Europe from the East. Most important, the United States has negotiated a free trade agreement with Mexico, and this goes well beyond anything now being offered by western to eastern Europe. This, in turn, is stimulating large private capital flows to Mexico, which is not reflected in the eastern European context.

This is a major difference between the United States and western Europe. The latter does not now contemplate full-fledged free trade with the migrant-sending countries of eastern Europe and the former Soviet Union. The other major difference is that while western Europe does receive many immigrants, the underlying philosophy is that the countries are not immigrant countries. The United States, by contrast, does consider itself an immigrant country and in fact receives many immigrants.

The immigration issue has taken on a strong political aspect in the main countries of western Europe. Anti-immigration positions are hardening in Germany, France, and Italy; the United Kingdom has long been opposed to immigration. The immigration problem in Europe will almost certainly not be resolved in the foreseeable future, certainly not as long as there is economic pressure for people to emigrate from eastern Europe and the countries of the former Soviet Union. The existence of this insoluble problem, however, may well alter the political lineup in the key countries of western Europe.

The political repercussions of unwanted immigration have until now been less severe in the United States, but this may be changing. The forces behind the change are the sheer numbers of these immigrants, coupled with recent acts of terrorism by persons who entered the United States as asylees, the evidence that once asylum claimants come under U.S. jurisdiction they can readily submerge themselves into the general population, plus the repeated instances of Chinese immigrants being smuggled into the country on unsafe ships.

Immigration issues are thus moving front and center on the political stage in both Europe and the United States in ways that presage greater restrictionism even as the numbers of potential emigrants increase. There is no short-term solution to this dilemma.

Notes

1.   These people may be wanted by their families, but generally not by the country of immigration. Even this overstates in that many asylees will later be granted permanent resident status. Yet the word *unwanted* seems appropriate.

2.   Philip L. Martin, *Trade and Migration: The Case of NAFTA* (Washington, D.C.: Institute for International Economics, 1993), gives the number of illegal foreigners in Japan at 300,000—a tenfold increase during the 1980s. This is still a relatively small number, 0.24 percent, in a country of about 125 million people.

3.   The clamor to "do something" about undocumented immigration subsided for a few years following the passage of the Immigration Reform and Control Act of 1986 (IRCA), but has risen again during the past few years. The issue was raised in the 1990 presidential campaign by Pat Buchanan when he sought the Republican nomination for president.

4.   Rodolfo O. de la Garza et al., *Latino Voices: Mexican, Puerto Rican, and Cuban Perspectives on American Politics* (Boulder: Westview Press, 1992), gives data on surveys showing that even most U.S. residents of Latin American origin oppose liberalized immigration.

5.   The figures in this paragraph come from data reported to the Continuous Reporting System on Migration (SOPEMI), Paris, Organization for Economic Cooperation and Development; and from *The Week in Germany*, a publication of the German Information Center in New York, January 22, 1993. Data on France in the next paragraph are from the submission by André Lebon for the 1991 SOPEMI report.

6.   Henry Kamm (*New York Times*, February 15, 1993, p. 1) described the smuggling of refugees by boat into Nordic countries, especially Sweden, from the former Yugoslavia, parts of the former Soviet Union, Somalia, other places in Africa, and Iraq (Kurds and others).

7.   See Sidney Weintraub, "Treating the Causes: Illegal Immigration and U.S. Foreign Economic Policy," in *The Unavoidable Issue: U.S. Immigration Policy in the 1980s*, ed. Demetrios Papademetriou and Mark J. Miller (Philadelphia: Institute for the Study of Human Issues, 1983), 185–214.

8.   An excellent example of this motive is the series of papers commissioned by the International Labor Organization and the United Nations High Commissioner for Refugees for a joint meeting in Geneva in 1992 on the theme of "International Aid as a Means to Reduce the Need for Emigration."

9.   The Report of the Commission for the Study of International Migration and Cooperative Economic Development, *Unauthorized Migration: An Economic Development Response* (Washington, D.C.: U.S. Government Printing Office, 1990), contained the following sentence: "This is our principal institutional message: that a government structure be designed to assure that the issue of migration policy receive as much attention as do the consuming but often transient day-to-day concerns that otherwise dominate the process" (p.

xv). The reason for this recommendation was that this was not the case. The CSIMCED was established pursuant to IRCA to examine how U.S. policy could affect the "push" factors in emigrant-sending countries.

10. Ibid., 3.

11. Douglas S. Massey, "Economic Development and International Migration in Comparative Perspective," in *Determinants of Emigration from Mexico, Central America, and the Caribbean,* ed. Sergio Diaz-Briquets and Sidney Weintraub (Boulder: Westview Press, 1991), 13–47.

12. Martin, *Trade and Migration. Maquiladoras* in other places are called export-processing zones. The bulk of these plants, upwards of 90 percent of the 2,000 *maquiladoras* that now exist, are located in Mexican cities along the U.S. border.

13. Raul Hinojosa-Ojeda and Sherman Robinson, "Alternative Scenarios of U.S.-Mexico Integration: A Computable General Equilibrium Approach," Working paper 609 (University of California, Berkeley, Department of Agricultural and Resource Economics, April 1991).

14. According to the Bank of Mexico, GDP growth in Mexico in recent years has been -3.8 percent in 1986, +1.7 percent in 1987, 1.2 percent in 1988, 3.3 percent in 1989, and 4.4 percent in 1990. Growth then slowed to 3.6 percent in 1991 and 2.6 percent in 1992.

15. Background on corn production can be found in Santiago Levy and Sweder van Wijnbergen, "Maize and the Mexico-United States Free Trade Agreement," Boston University and the World Bank, Washington, D.C., January 1991; and Levy and Wijnbergen, "Mexican Agriculture at the Crossroads," unpublished paper, January 1992.

16. See Mario M. Carrillo Huerta, "The Impact of *Maquiladoras* on Migration in Mexico," in *The Effects of Receiving Country Policies on Migration Flows,* ed. Sergio Diaz-Briquets and Sidney Weintraub (Boulder: Westview Press, 1991), 67–102.

17. Migration is obviously affected by more than economics. Once a migratory process starts, the formation of networks in sending and receiving countries keeps the process going. There is a chain reaction from family reunification, as is already happening as a result of the U.S. and European legalization programs. The European and U.S. guest-worker programs stimulated a chain reaction of migration for purposes of family reunification. The refugee flows are brought on by wars and deep uncertainty in sending areas. However, NAFTA is an economic initiative, and the relevant analysis for the purpose of this paper is economic.

18. Data in this paragraph are from the U.S. Department of Labor, Bureau of Labor Statistics, "International Comparisons of Hourly Compensation Costs for Production Workers in Manufacturing, 1991," Report 825, Washington, D.C., June 1992.

19. Francisco Alba, "The Mexican Demographic Situation," in *Mexican and Central American Population and U.S. Immigration Policy,* ed. Frank D. Bean, Jurgen Schmandt, and Sidney Weintraub (Austin, Texas: Center for Mexican American Studies, University of Texas at Austin, 1989), 5–32, provides data on demographic developments in Mexico.

20. The figure for the informal economy comes from a joint study of the Mexican Secretariat of Labor and Social Welfare and the U.S. Department of Labor, *The Informal Sector in Mexico*, Occasional Paper No. 1, September 1992.

21. See Peter Gregory, "The Determinants of International Migration and Policy Options for Influencing the Size of Population Flows," in *Determinants of Emigration*.

22. Data in this paragraph are from the U.S. Immigration and Naturalization Service, *Statistical Yearbook of the Immigration and Naturalization Service, 1991* (Washington, D.C.: U.S. Government Printing Office, 1992).

23. Anthony P. Maingot, ed., *Small Country Development and International Labor Flows: Experiences in the Caribbean* (Boulder: Westview Press, 1991), 4.

24. The most important of these products where tariff barriers in the United States are still high are clothing and apparel, footwear and other leather products, canned tuna, and watches incorporating parts originating in a communist country. See DeLisle Worrell, "U.S.-Caricom Free Trade," in *The Premise and the Promise: Free Trade in the Americas*, ed. Sylvia Saborio (New Brunswick, N.J.: Transaction/Overseas Development Council, 1992), 226.

25. See Sidney Weintraub and Sergio Diaz-Briquets, "The Use of Foreign Aid to Reduce Incentives to Emigrate from Central America," Working per (World Employment Program, International Labour Office, Geneva, February 1992).

26. Three reports from the Center for Strategic and International Studies s attention on these issues: Georges A. Fauriol, ed., *The Haitian Challenge* (93); Ernest H. Preeg with Jonathan D. Levine, *Cuba and the New Caribbean Economic Order* (1993); and Georges A. Fauriol, ed., *U.S.-Caribbean Relations into the Twenty-First Century* (forthcoming 1994).

27. Preeg and Levine, *Cuba*, 56–57.

28. Richard Layard, Olivier Blanchard, Rudiger Dornbusch, and Paul Krugman, *East-West Migration: The Alternatives* (Cambridge: MIT Press, 1992), 2.

For information about other CSIS publications, contact:

CSISBOOKS
1800 K Street, N.W.
Suite 400
Washington, D.C.   20006

Telephone   202-775-3119
Facsimile   202-775-3199